Paper Industry in India

Production Structure and Productivity Growth

PAPER INDUSTRY IN INDIA

Production Structure and Productivity Growth

Kaustuva Barik

ABHIJEET PUBLICATIONS
DELHI 110 094

ABHIJEET PUBLICATIONS
2/46 Tukhmeerpur Extension
Delhi-110 094
Phone: 2218 1492
e-mail: abhijeet_singh@vsnl.net

PAPER INDUSTRY IN INDIA: PRODUCTION STRUCTURE AND PRODUCTIVITY GROWTH

First Published 2003

ISBN 81-88683-11-6

PRINTED IN INDIA

Published by J.K. Singh for Abhijeet Publications, Delhi 110 094; Lasertypeset by Abhijeet Typesetters, Delhi, and Printed at Tarun Offset Printers, Delhi.

Preface

Measured productivity growth obtained through the Solow residual may be at variance with pure technological change in an industry when standard assumptions such as constant returns to scale, full utilisation of capacity and perfect competition in the product market are not fulfilled. In such cases estimated TFP needs to be adjusted for scale economies, capacity utilisation and mark-up over marginal costs so as to obtain a measure of technological change in the industry. The present book is an attempt in this direction. Using annual aggregate data of the Indian paper industry, it presents estimates of a translog variable cost function and production structure of the industry.

An important finding is that traditional TFP and TFP adjusted for scale economies, capacity utilisation and mark-up have moved in opposite directions during the period 1973-98. While traditional TFP registered a decreasing trend over the study period, technological change is found to have recorded a positive growth. The negative growth rate in TFP of the Indian paper industry is coupled with presence of economies of scale and under-utilisation of capacity and substantial mark-up over marginal cost. These features make TFP a poor representative of technological change and bring in a downward bias into it. After purging the effects of scale economies, capacity utilisation and mark-up from TFP growth, a positive trend in the residual is obtained.

The book is based largely on my doctoral dissertation at the Indian Institute of technology, Delhi. During the course of research I have benefited substantially from a number of persons. Prof. V. Upadhyay has been very helpful and a guiding force. I have benefited from discussions with Prof. Gopinath Pradhan, my colleague at IGNOU.

Thanks are due to Prof. D.N. Rao for his valuable help in solving the equilibrium level of capital stock by numerical iteration. Prof. K. L. Krishna has been kind enough to offer suggestions whenever needed. I am thankful to Prof. Frank T. Denton and Prof. M. N. Murty for their valuable comments. Dr. Hrushikesh Panda provided encouragement and important suggestions during my interaction with him. Prof. Tapas Sen and Mr. V. Selvaraju have been of tremendous help.

My colleagues at IGNOU, particularly Prof. Kapil Kumar, Dr. Debal Singha Roy and Mr. Saugato Sen have offered help at various stages of the study.

I am thankful to my wife Koushalya for her patience and unfailing support during research and writing of the book. My family members have been quite encouraging throughout.

I am solely responsible for the remaining errors.*

Kaustuva Barik

*Publisher also shares the burden with author.

Contents

Part I
Production Structure

1

Introduction

Why This Study?

The paper industry is the second industry to be liberalised in India after the cement industry. Much before the liberalisation euphoria of the 1990s, the paper industry was partially delicensed in 1984-85, particularly the agro-based paper mills segment. Delicensing was extended to other segments of the industry in 1991. Thus the industry has witnessed radical policy changes starting from a command and controlled policy regime to a liberalised one. These changes have affected various fields of operations and given a more flexible approach to decision making. As a result, the industry is expected to improve upon its productivity performance under a liberalised regime compared to a command and control one.

Second, the demand for paper in India has persistently been higher than its supply. To bridge the demand-supply gap, many concessions have been offered to the industry, besides delicensing. These concessions include liberalised imports of pulp and waste paper (1982), import of second hand machinery (1974), excise rebates on use of unconventional raw material (1982), extension of the concept of broad-banding (1984) and removal of statutory control over production, pricing and distribution of white printing paper (1987). These changes are expected to have influenced the production structure and productivity of the industry.

Third, although the Indian paper industry has witnessed rapid growth in level of output, number of production units and variety of paper and paper products over the years, analysis of its productivity performance has been at a rudimentary level. While the number of paper mills at the beginning of the planning era in India, i.e., 1950-51, was only 17, presently this number has gone up to 380. Simultaneously the installed capacity of the industry has increased from a meagre 0.135 million tonnes per annum (tpa) in 1950-51 to 4.6 million tpa in 1998-99. While production in the industry was limited to a small variety of paper products in the beginning, product diversification took place over the years and by the year 1990 the paper industry was self sufficient in most varieties of paper except in newsprint.

Fourth, the production process in the paper industry is energy intensive with the energy bill constituting approximately 20 per cent of variable cost. With the global rise in oil prices, there have been efforts to cut down expenditure on fuel consumption at every level. Innovation in paper production technology, from chemical based to thermo-mechanical, is expected to improve efficiency in the industry but is yet to be examined empirically.

Fifth, paper production makes intensive use of forest-based raw material, which is undergoing a decrease in supply. Keeping such scarcity in view the government has encouraged establishment of small plants based on agro-residue. Even then, shortage of non-energy raw material remains a sore point for the industry. Under such circumstances long-run sustainability of the industry depends, to a large extent, on the efficiency with which scarce resources are utilised.

Sixth, in recent years there have been reports of declining rates of capacity utilisation and profitability [see various issues of Report on Currency and Finance, RBI]. Recently the problem has reached to the extent of non-viability and closure of many firms. For example, 6 integrated units and 67 small and medium units accounting for 20 per cent of total installed capacity in the industry remained closed during 1987-88 [RBI 1988]. The problem, which started during the mid-1980s, has continued to the present [*The Economic Times*, May 17, 1999].

These factors call for an analysis of the production structure and productivity of the industry. For analysing production structure four characteristics are considered, viz., rate of capacity utilisation, returns to scale, mark-up over marginal cost, and substitution elasticities among inputs. On the other hand, productivity growth in the industry is analysed through estimation of total factor productivity (TFP). Detailed analysis of these characteristics of the industry would throw light on the above features of the industry.

In view of the above we analyse the production structure and the pattern of growth in productivity in the case of the paper industry of India. For this purpose we consider total factor productivity (TFP) which takes into account all inputs used in the production of output. TFP is a broad measure of productivity in which factors such as non-constant returns to scale, mark-up and capacity utilisation get lumped in with technological progress. Hence we attempt to purge the effects of these factors from TFP so that technological progress in the industry is isolated. With this broad framework, we

- examine the production structure of the industry through an econometric estimation of *(i)* scale economies, *(ii)* capacity utilisation, *(iii)* mark-up over marginal cost, and *(iv)* substitution elasticities,
- estimate the trend in TFP growth and identify any change in it during the post-liberalisation period, and
- isolate technological change from TFP growth by purging the effects of scale economies, capacity utilisation and mark-up.

Major Policy Developments in Indian Paper Industry

The Indian paper industry, as observed above, has operated in an excess demand environment for its products for most of the time [Ahuja 1992]. In order to manage the problem of shortages the government has adopted a three-pronged strategy: *(i)* devise policies to contain the demand for paper, *(ii)* augment the supply of paper and paper products, and *(iii)* bridge the gap between demand and supply by imports. While use of the first strategy has declined over time, efforts towards augmenting supply are being continued.

The restrictions on production, distribution and pricing were imposed mainly through paper control orders. They ranged from limiting the consumption of some products (e.g., curtailing number of pages in journals and ratio of imported newsprint) to imposing a ban on production of certain products (e.g., diary, calendar, cards, etc.). Under the Paper Control Order, 1974, paper mills were required to devote 30 per cent of their production to white printing paper. Not only that, the industry was required to sell 25 per cent of its writing paper to the government at a concessional rate.

In an effort to augment supply, the government *(i)* encouraged establishment of smaller production units, particularly those using non-conventional raw materials such as bagasse and agro-residue, *(ii)* allowed import of second hand technology, and *(iii)* allowed unrestricted import of paper grade pulp.

Despite such efforts the industry has not been able to close the gap between supply and demand through domestic production and import of paper and paper products is frequently resorted to. The gap is alarming in the field of newsprint, as approximately 40 per cent of newsprint requirement in India is met through imports. The value of imports (in Rupee terms) as a percentage of domestic production has varied between 17.5 percent in 1980 and 8.2 percent in 1992 while the average over the period 1973-98 has been 11.8 percent.

The excess demand condition has bestowed the producers with an assured demand for their products. In fact, existing firms in the industry have enjoyed a couple of advantages, particularly during the controlled policy regime, which continued up to the early 1980s. First, protection from external competition was offered to the industry on grounds of import substitution and foreign exchange conservation. A high rate of tariff and quantitative restrictions on imports were imposed in this period. The collection rate of import duty on the paper industry was to the extent of 24 per cent during the year 1990-91, after which there was a decline. At present paper products are subjected to an import duty of 8 percent. On the other hand, quantitative restrictions in the industry were imposed in the form of issue of special import licenses on an annual basis. A typical example is the case of newsprint imports. Imported newsprint being cheaper than domestically produced newsprint, domestic producers were facing a real challenge. In order to protect domestic producers the government imposed restrictions such that big newspaper houses could import newsprint up to 70 per cent of their total consumption while at least 30 per cent consumption was stipulated to be domestic. Secondly, rigorous licensing policy imposed barriers on entry into the industry, which reduced competition from potential domestic investors. An entry-barrier for potential competitors was induced by the policy, which helped existing firms to operate in an insulated market without looking into technological developments or production costs [Ahluwalia 1985]. Although domestic production increased, it also promoted inefficiency in the production process. In the face of depleting raw material reserves and rising energy prices, the industry could not continue to be cost-effective, especially in its intermediate input bill. In such production environment the rate of growth in productivity, which reflects the rate of diminution in production costs, is expected to be negligible or even negative.

The extensive use of raw material and energy in the production process by the Indian paper industry has generated the problem of air and water pollution. According to the Central Pollution Control Board (CPCB) of India, the paper industry is one of the seventeen most polluting industries in the country. In order to lessen the pollution problem the government has undertaken regulatory measures in the form of the Water Act (1974), Air Act (1981) and Environment Act (1986). These measures required the industries to comply with emission standards and pollution abatement technology.

The pollution control measures have affected the production environment of the Indian paper industry. Earlier the paper mills, usually set up on the banks of water streams, were in a position to leave its unprocessed effluent into the water streams. As a result, the mills could save some costs on the processing of the discharge, although at the cost of environment. With declaration of the stricter pollution laws, the industry has been forced to go for pollution abatement technology. The new technology, however, has the benefit of not only reducing pollution, but also improving the productivity of the industry [World Bank, 1992].

In order to increase the production, public policy shifted

during the 1980s towards encouragement of small-scale units, particularly those using at least 75% raw material from non-conventional sources such as bagasse and agro-residue. These units were not only de-licensed but also offered concessions in excise duties. Such a policy served three purposes: one, it helped in reducing regional inequalities in paper production; two, it helped in generation of additional employment; and three, it ameliorated to some extent the problem of raw material shortage. However, problems related to viability and scale economies were soon to be encountered. During the year 1999-2000, unviable units accounting for about 20 per cent of installed capacity in the industry remained closed [*The Economic Times*, May 17, 1999]. Major factors behind such a feature were pointed out to be non-viability, obsolete technology, labour unrest, inadequate supply of raw material and power, and unviable capacity utilisation [RBI (a)].

Organisation of the Book

The book is organised into nine chapters including the present one spread over two parts. The first part deals with the production structure in the industry while the second part covers the growth rate in productivity and its contribution to output growth.

Chapter 2, which follows, presents the theoretical framework for undertaking a study of the present nature. It deals with the method adopted for estimation of capacity utilisation, returns to scale, mark-up over marginal cost, substitution elasticities among inputs. Chapter 3 outlines the data source and construction of variable in order to carry out empirical estimation of the production characteristics dealt in the previous chapter. Chapter 4 provides empirical results and their implications for policy analysis.

Chapter 5 brings out the approaches to productivity measurement while Chapter 6 presents preliminary results. In chapter 7 the methods of analysis and empirical results on the contribution of productivity to output growth are discussed. Chapter 8 isolates technological progress by purging the effects of capacity utilisation, scale economies and mark-up from traditional productivity estimate. Chapter 9 brings out the major conclusions of the study.

2

Theoretical Framework

A framework for estimation of important characteristics indicating the production structure requires the specification of a structure for technology in the industry. This specification could take the form of either a production function or its dual, cost function. There is a general preference for the use of a cost function rather than the production or price function. The underlying reasons for such preference are spelt out later in Chapter 5.

We assume that the industry utilises four inputs, viz., capital (*K*), labour (*L*), energy (*E*) and raw material (*M*) in the production of output (*Y*). Of the inputs, three are variable (*L*, *E* and *M*) in the sense that their levels can be varied in the short-run. The remaining variable, *K*, is assumed to be quasi-fixed such that its level can be changed only in the long-run, not in the short-run. This gives a partial static equilibrium (PSE) framework[1] to our analysis and requires the specification of a variable cost function. The econometric estimation of a variable cost function within a PSE framework allows us to obtain estimates of capacity utilisation, scale economies, mark-up over marginal cost, and substitution elasticities among inputs. In the section that follows we specify a variable cost function along with required properties.

Translog Variable Cost Function

We employ a translog variable cost function, which is one of the widely used flexible functional forms. This functional form imposes minimum restrictions on technology and is a second order approximation to an arbitrary function. It allows yearly variation in CU and scale economies. Moreover, it allows for variation in substitution elasticities across observations as well as pairs of inputs. Before presenting the equation used for estimation in the study we give the formulation of the translog cost function[2] in general. This is given by

$$\ln C = \beta_0 + \sum_i \beta_i \ln P_i + \frac{1}{2}\sum_i\sum_j \beta_{ij} \ln P_i \ln P_j + \beta_Y \ln Y + \frac{1}{2}\beta_{YY}(\ln Y)^2 + \sum_i \beta_{iY} \ln Y \ln P_i$$
$$+ \sum_i \beta_{it} \ln P_i t + \beta_{Yt} \ln Y t + \beta_t t + \frac{1}{2}\beta_{tt} t^2 \quad (i = K, L, E, M) \qquad \text{...(2.1)}$$

In (2.1) all the inputs are variable and adjust to their equilibrium levels within a single time period, which characterizes a full static equilibrium (FSE) framework. Theoretically it is necessary that a cost function should be linear homogeneous in input prices. That has the implication that a proportionate increase in input prices increases cost by the same proportion. The translog cost function as specified at (2.1) does not satisfy such linear homogeneity conditions. For the fulfillment of these, additional restrictions are to be imposed on the parameters of (2.1). These restrictions are as follows:

$$\sum_i \beta_i = 1; \quad \sum_i \beta_{ij} = \sum_i \beta_{iy} = \sum_i \beta_{it} = 0; \quad \beta_{ij} = \beta_{ji} \qquad \text{...(2.2)}$$

Specification of Translog Variable Cost Function

In the short-run the firm takes into account the variable cost, not the total cost. Moreover, the price of *K* does not play any role in deciding the level of *K*, as its level cannot be changed. Thus what enters into the variable cost specification[3] is the level of the capital stock.

For the translog specification, when a firm is using three variable inputs (*L*, *E*, *M*) and one quasi-fixed input (*K*), the short-run variable cost function is given as follows[4]:

$$\ln VC = \beta_0 + \beta_Y \ln Y + \sum_i \beta_i \ln P_i + \beta_K \ln K + \frac{1}{2}\beta_{YY}(\ln Y)^2 + \frac{1}{2}\sum_i\sum_j \beta_{ij} \ln P_i \ln P_j$$
$$+ \frac{1}{2}\beta_{KK}(\ln K)^2 + \sum_i \beta_{iY} \ln Y \ln P_i + \sum_i \beta_{ik} \ln K \ln P_i + \beta_{KY} \ln K \ln Y$$
$$+ \sum_i \beta_{it} \ln P_i\, t + \beta_{Yt} \ln Y\, t + \beta_t t + \frac{1}{2}\beta_{tt} t^2 + \beta_{Kt} \ln K\, t$$
$$(i, j = L, E, M) \qquad \text{...(2.3)}$$

The translog short-run variable cost function at (2.3) is homogeneous of degree one in input prices if the following restrictions are fulfilled:

$$\sum_i \beta_i = 1; \quad \sum_i \beta_{ij} = \sum_i \beta_{iy} = \sum_i \beta_{it} = \sum_i \beta_{ik} = 0; \quad \beta_{ij} = \beta_{ji} \qquad \text{...(2.4)}$$

The input demand functions have a separate identity and can be easily derived from the cost function. In a translog formulation we obtain factor share equations (implying factor demand) by logarithmic differentiation with respect to variable input prices and applying Shephard's lemma[5] as follows:

$$\frac{\partial \ln VC}{\partial \ln P_i} = S_i = \beta_i + \sum_j \beta_{ij} \ln P_j + \beta_{iK} \ln K + \beta_{iY} \ln Y + \beta_{it} t \qquad \text{...(2.5)}$$

$$(i = L, E, M)$$

where S_i is the ith share equation[6]. It may be noted that the factor share equations should be homogeneous of degree zero. This implies that a proportionate increase in input prices does not change the equilibrium level of input requirements. These share equations need to be estimated together with the cost function to gain greater efficiency in estimation.

Curvature Conditions

The estimated variable cost function specified at (2.3) is expected to be consistent with theory and thus should fulfil certain conditions. The estimated variable cost function should be *(i)* non-decreasing in variable factor prices, *(ii)* non-increasing in quasi-fixed factors, *(iii)* non-decreasing in output, *(iv)* homogeneous of degree one in variable input prices, *(v)* concave in variable input prices, and *(vi)* convex in quasi-fixed factors [Hazilla and Kopp 1986]. These consistency properties are expressed in terms of the derivatives of the cost function and given in Table 2.1.

Estimation of a translog cost function with empirical data may not satisfy the above consistency properties globally. According to Lau (1986), '...however, even when global theoretical consistency fails, there is still a set of prices of inputs over which theoretical consistency holds and this set may well be large enough for all practical purposes'.

Table 2.1
Theoretical Consistency Properties of the Variable Cost Function

Property	*Description*	*Derivatives*
1	Non-decreasing in P_i	$\partial VC/\partial P_i \geq 0$
2	Non-increasing in K	$\partial VC/\partial K \leq 0$
3	Non-decreasing in Y	$\partial VC/\partial Y \geq 0$
4	Homogeneous of degree one in P_i	$\sum_i (\partial VC/\partial P_i)P_i = VC$
5	Variable factor symmetry	$\partial^2 VC/\partial P_i\, \partial P_j = \partial^2 VC/\partial P_j\, \partial P_i$
6	Concave in P_i	$\begin{bmatrix} \partial^2 VC/\partial P_L^2 & \partial^2 VC/\partial P_L \partial P_E & \partial^2 VC/\partial P_L \partial P_M \\ \partial^2 VC/\partial P_L \partial P_E & \partial^2 VC/\partial P_E^2 & \partial^2 VC/\partial P_E \partial P_M \\ \partial^2 VC/\partial P_L \partial P_M & \partial^2 VC/\partial P_E \partial P_M & \partial^2 VC/\partial P_M^2 \end{bmatrix}$ is negative semi-definite
7	Convex in K	$\partial^2 VC/\partial K^2 \geq 0$

Note: The above table is based on Hazilla and Kopp (1986).

As can be seen from Table 2.1 these consistency properties of the cost function are both of equality and inequality types. While the equality type restrictions are easy to impose on the cost function at the estimation stage, the non-linear type poses some problem because of requisite computer software. Hence, of the properties given in Table 2.1, properties 4-5 are imposed at the estimation stage while properties 1-3 and 6-7 are tested on the estimated cost function at every observation.

From the list of properties given in the table it may be noted that properties 4 & 5 hold good if the restrictions specified at (2.4) are imposed on the translog variable cost function at the estimation stage. Regarding the other properties we discuss below:

With respect to property 1 in Table 2.1, it is equivalent to the condition that the estimated factor shares be non-negative. In (2.5) since both *VC* and P_i are non-negative, $\frac{\partial VC}{\partial P_i} \geq 0 \Rightarrow \frac{\partial VC}{\partial P_i}\frac{P_i}{VC} \geq 0 \Rightarrow \frac{\partial \ln VC}{\partial \ln P_i} \geq 0$. By applying Shephard's lemma we know that $\frac{\partial \ln VC}{\partial \ln P_i} = \frac{\partial VC}{\partial P_i}\frac{P_i}{VC} = \frac{P_i X_i}{VC} = S_i$. Thus the property that the variable cost function should be monotonically increasing in input prices is fulfilled if estimated shares for the variable inputs are found to be positive at all data points.

Properties 2, 3 and 7 are directly tested by the estimated variable cost function. The equations taken for assessment of these properties are as follows:

Property 2:

Since $\frac{\partial VC}{\partial K} = \frac{K}{VC}\frac{\partial \ln VC}{\partial \ln K}$ and *VC* and *K* are non-negative, the cost function is decreasing in *K* if $\frac{\partial \ln VC}{\partial \ln K}$ is non-positive. From (2.3) we see that

$$\frac{\partial \ln VC}{\partial \ln K} = \beta_K + \beta_{KK} \ln K + \sum_i \beta_{iK} \ln P_i + \beta_{KY} \ln Y + \beta_{Kt} t \qquad ...(2.6)$$

Thus, the property that the estimated cost function is decreasing in *K* is fulfilled if (2.6) is found to be non-positive.

Property 3:

Similar to the above, property 3 holds good if $\frac{\partial \ln VC}{\partial \ln Y} \geq 0$ since *VC* and *Y* are non-negative. By logarithmic partial differentiation of (2.3) we have

$$\frac{\partial \ln VC}{\partial \ln Y} = \beta_Y + \beta_{YY} \ln Y + \sum_i \beta_{iY} \ln P_i + \beta_{YK} \ln K + \beta_{Yt} t \qquad ...(2.7)$$

We find (2.7) by combining appropriate parameter estimates and property 3 is fulfilled if the estimated values are non-negative at all observations.

Property 7:

This property is derived from (2.3) by taking second order partial derivatives with respect to *K*. Moreover, this condition is fulfilled if $\frac{\partial^2 \ln VC}{\partial \ln K^2} = \beta_{KK} \geq 0$. Thus we evaluate the estimated coefficient of the parameter β_{KK} for non-negativity.

Property 6:

A necessary and sufficient condition for a twice continuously differentiable cost function to be concave in input prices over the positive orthant is negative semi-definiteness of the Hessian matrix. The logarithmic second order derivatives of the variable cost function are related to ordinary first and second order derivatives by the following identity [Diewert and Wales 1987].

$$\frac{\partial^2 \ln VC}{\partial \ln P_i \partial \ln P_j} = \frac{\delta_{ij} P_i C_i}{C} - \frac{P_i P_j C_i C_j}{C^2} + \frac{P_i P_j C_{ij}}{C} \quad \text{...(2.8)}$$

where $\delta_{ij} = 1$ if $i = j$
$= 0$ if $i \neq j$;

$C_i = \frac{\partial VC(.)}{\partial P_i}$ and

$C_{ij} = \frac{\partial^2 VC(.)}{\partial P_i \partial P_j}$.

Since the left-hand side of (2.8) is equal to the parameter β_{ij}, the Hessian matrix reduces to

$$H = A - S + \hat{S}\hat{S}' \quad \text{...(2.9)}$$

where *H* is the Hessian matrix

A is the $n \times n$ parameter matrix with β_{ij} coefficients in the main diagonal,

S is the $n \times n$ matrix with factor shares in the diagonal, and

$\hat{S}$ is the factor share vector [Diewert and Wales 1987].

We evaluate matrix (2.9) at each observation so as to check for its semi-definiteness.

Validity of Hicks-neutrality, Homotheticity and Homogeneity

The variable cost function specified at (2.3) includes a number of parameters which reflect interaction between exogenous variables. Specific combinations of these interactive terms portray certain features of production structure such as Hicks-neutrality, homotheticity and homogeneity. Presence of these features in the production structure is tested by imposing appropriate restrictions on the cost function (2.3) and assessing the validity of such restrictions.

The presence of Hicks-neutrality, homotheticity and homogeneity in (2.3) are tested through the likelihood ratio test following Christensen and Greene (1976). This test procedure involves three steps: First, we estimate the cost function (2.3) without imposing any restriction regarding the features mentioned above, viz., Hicks-neutrality, homotheticity and homogeneity. Second, we re-estimate the cost function with the required restrictions imposed. In the third step, we compare the maximum value of the likelihood function in both the estimations (without and with restrictions) and work out the likelihood ratio statistic (λ) as follows:

$$\lambda = -2(\ln R - \ln U) \qquad ...(2.10)$$

where R and U refer to the value assumed by the likelihood function 'with restriction' and 'without restriction' respectively. In this procedure λ follows (asymptotically) a chi-squared distribution with degree of freedom equal to the number of independent restrictions imposed at the second stage.

In order to test the validity of Hicks-neutrality, homotheticity and homogeneity we impose restrictions as follows:

$$\text{Hicks-neutrality: } \beta_{Lt} = \beta_{Et} = \beta_{Mt} = \beta_{Kt} = 0 \qquad ...(2.11)$$

$$\text{Homotheticity: } \beta_{LY} = \beta_{EY} = \beta_{MY} = \beta_{KY} = 0 \qquad ...(2.12)$$

$$\text{Homogeneity: } \beta_{LY} = \beta_{EY} = \beta_{MY} = \beta_{KY} = \beta_{YY} = 0 \qquad ...(2.13)$$

The λ value obtained according to (2.11) in the case of Hicks-neutrality has an asymptotic chi-squared distribution with three degrees of freedom, as there are three independent restrictions. As we see from (2.4) the restriction $\beta_{Lt} = \beta_{Et} = 0$ automatically makes the third coefficient $\beta_{Mt} = 0$ because of the condition $\Sigma\beta_{it} = 0$ required for linear homogeneity in input prices. Similarly, the numbers of independent restrictions for homotheticity and homogeneity are 3 and 4 respectively. On the basis of a comparison between the tabulated value and actual value we can decide on whether to use (2.3) or its truncated form by restricting some parameters to be zero.

Economic Capacity Utilisation

The rate of capacity utilisation is inherently built into the PSE model. Here it is assumed that the industry is not in a position to adjust the level of capital to its equilibrium level in the short-run. Thus in the case of shortfall in demand and consequent decline in output, the level of the capital stock cannot be reduced immediately. This results in under-utilisation of the existing capacity. Similarly when increased demand warrants expansion of capital stock but short-run rigidity does not allow it, the industry has to manage with over-utilisation of existing capital stock. Thus CU can be on either side of unity, which is in sharp contrast to traditional CU measures which are always less than unity. Moreover, the problem of CU in this framework is essentially a short-run phenomenon.

In terms of concepts from economic theory it was Cassels (1937) who defined capacity output as that level of output where the long-run average cost (LRAC) curve is minimum [Berndt and Hesse 1986]. Such an idea is based on the equilibrium condition that the short-run average cost (SRAC) curve is tangent to the LRAC curve in the long-run under perfect competition. However, in the short-run a 'temporary equilibrium' [Berndt and Fuss 1986] is possible at any point on the SRAC curve, depending upon the placement of the demand curve. In this framework the industry may reap the benefits of scale economies or suffer diseconomies in the short-run but in the long run there is constant returns to scale (CRTS).

In case the industry does not fulfill the CRTS condition capacity output is defined as that level of output where SRAC and LRAC curves are tangent [Klein 1960]. In this framework, the industry deviates from long-run equilibrium whenever its input-output bundle does not correspond to a point on the LRAC curve [Berndt and Fuss 1986].

Conceptual Framework

In a PSE framework the industry is in equilibrium when SRAC and LRAC curves are tangent to each other. The output level at such a tangency point is defined as the optimum output for the industry [Klein 1960]. The rate of CU, in such a framework, is given by the ratio of actual output to capacity output. Alternatively, in terms of a cost function it is the ratio of shadow cost to actual cost. Thus we have two CU measures: primal and dual. The primal CU measure is defined as

$$CU_q = \frac{Y}{Y^*} \qquad \text{...(2.14)}$$

where CU_q is the primal CU measure, Y is actual output and Y^* is capacity output. Similarly, dual CU measure is defined as

$$CU_C = \frac{C^*}{C} \qquad \text{...(2.15)}$$

where CU_C is the cost CU measure, $C = VC + P_K K$ is the actual cost of production and $C^* = VC + P_K K^*$ is the shadow cost. Here K^* refers to the equilibrium level of capital stock[7]. Alternatively the shadow cost is given by $C^* = \sum_i P_i X_i + Z_K K$ where Z_K is the shadow price of capital[8].

Since it is possible to depict the short-run phenomenon explicitly through a variable cost function we derive both primal and dual CU measures from the cost function itself.

Primal CU Measure

In the short run the industry minimises total variable cost given that K is fixed at a particular level, say, $\overline{K}$. On the other hand, K is variable in the long-run and adjusts to its equilibrium level,

K^*. In the long-run there is no tendency on the part of the industry to change the equilibrium level of capital stock unless there are changes in level of output, variable input prices or technology.

It is useful to note that the tangency between SRAC and LRAC curves takes place at the level of output where SRMC and LRMC are equal. While equating SRMC to LRMC the industry considers variable cost $VC = G(Y, P_i, K, t)$ in the short-run. Here marginal cost is given by

$$SRMC = \left.\frac{dG}{dY}\right|_{K=\bar{K}} = \frac{\partial G}{\partial Y} \qquad \text{...(2.16)}$$

In the long-run, however, the prime concern of the industry is the total cost curve $TC = C(Y, P, t)$ where all inputs, including K, are variable. Thus $C = G + P_K \cdot K$ and LRMC is given by [Morrison 1988c]

$$LRMC = \frac{dC}{dY} = \frac{dG}{dY} + P_K\left(\frac{dK}{dY}\right)$$

$$= \frac{\partial G}{\partial Y} + \frac{\partial G}{\partial K} \cdot \frac{dK}{dY} + P_K\left(\frac{dK}{dY}\right) \qquad \text{...(2.17)}$$

On equating (2.16) and (2.17) we get

$$\frac{\partial G}{\partial K} \cdot \frac{dK}{dY} + P_K\left(\frac{dK}{dY}\right) = 0$$

or, $$\left(\frac{\partial G}{\partial K} + P_K\right)\frac{dK}{dY} = 0$$

or, $$-Z_K = P_K \qquad \text{...(2.18)}$$

where $Z_K = -\dfrac{\partial G}{\partial K}$ is the shadow price of capital [Lau 1978] and

P_K is the one-period market rental of capital. Thus full equilibrium is achieved when the shadow price of capital is equal to its one period market rental.

When the industry is not in equilibrium, $Z_K \neq P_K$ and two distinct cases emerge: *(i)* $Z_K > P_K$, and *(ii)* $Z_K < P_K$. In the first case the industry perceives the intrinsic (shadow) value of existing capital to be higher than its market value. Consequently, the industry utilises existing capital more than optimum. In this situation CU_q returns a value greater than unity. On the other hand, when $Z_K < P_K$ the industry perceives the intrinsic value of existing capital to be less than its market value. As a result existing capital is under-utilised and excess capacity exists.

From the translog short-run variable cost function we are in a position to obtain $\frac{\partial \ln G}{\partial \ln K}$ by taking logarithmic partial derivative with respect to *K* such that[9]

$$\frac{\partial \ln G}{\partial \ln K} = \beta_K + \beta_{KK} \ln K + \beta_{KL} \ln(P_L/P_M) + \beta_{KE} \ln(P_E/P_M) + \beta_{KY} \ln Y + \beta_{Kt} t \quad ...(2.19)$$

From (2.19) we obtain $-\frac{\partial G}{\partial K}$ and equate it with P_K such that

$$-\frac{VC}{K}(\beta_K + \beta_{KK} \ln K + \beta_{KL} \ln(P_L/P_M) + \beta_{KE} \ln(P_E/P_M) + \beta_{KY} \ln Y + \beta_{Kt} t) = P_K \quad ...(2.20)$$

From (2.20) we find the equilibrium quantity of output (Y^*) by solving it for given levels of capital stock (*K*) and input prices. Once Y^* is obtained, estimation of CU_q is straightforward using (2.14).

Dual CU Measure

The cost CU measure, CU_C, is obtained from the translog variable cost function, in a manner similar to CU_q. However, unlike the uniqueness of CU_q, the definition of CU_C contains some ambiguity as there are at least two different measures of CU_C, viz., average cost CU_C and shadow cost CU_C [Morrison 1988c]. Although these two measures are structurally equivalent, there is some conceptual difference between the two. This can be explained by means of two diagrams borrowed from Morrison (1988c) as shown in Fig. 2.1 and Fig. 2.2.

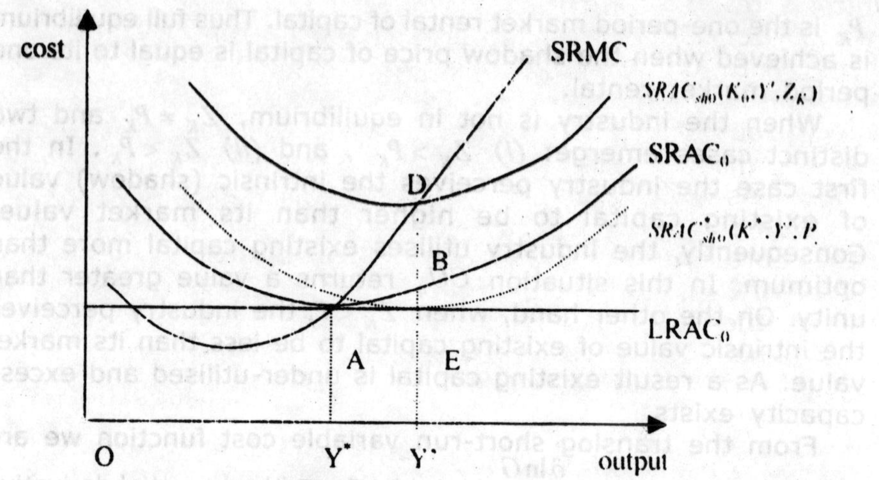

Fig. 2.1

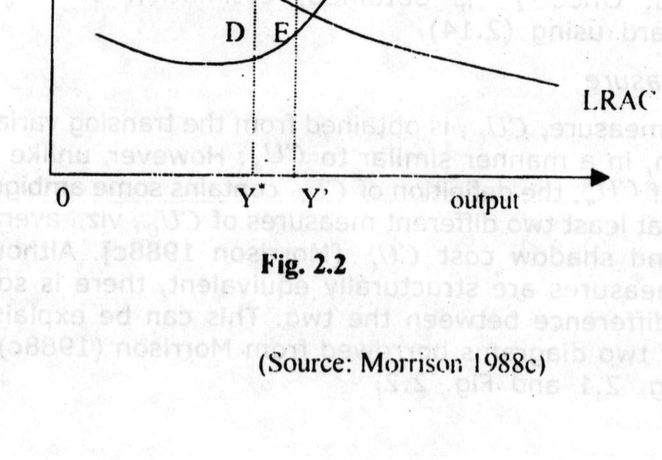

Fig. 2.2

(Source: Morrison 1988c)

In Fig. 2.1 we assume long-run CRTS for simpler exposition which is relaxed later in Fig. 2.2. In Fig. 2.1, LRAC is given by a horizontal straight line because of long-run CRTS. In the short-run the industry operates with capital stock K_0, which influences short-run average cost curve $SRAC_0$ and optimum capacity output for $SRAC_0$, Y^*. Let us consider the output level Y' which the industry produces keeping in view market demand. As $Y' > Y^*$ (see Fig. 2.1) there is a requirement for expansion of *K* from its existing level K_0 which is not feasible in the short-run. Thus the industry perceives the shadow price of capital, Z_k, to be higher than its market rental P_K. In the process, the industry revaluates its existing capital stock K_0 so that the short-run average shadow cost function shifts to $SRAC_{sh\,0}(K_0, Y', Z_K)$ with minimum point at Y'. In the long-run, when K_0 increases to K^*, the equality between market rental and shadow price is regained and the shadow cost function slides downward to $SRAC^*_{sh\,0}(K^*, Y', P_K)$

In the above frame of analysis, identification of both the cost CU measures is in order. The shadow cost CU_C measure is given by $\frac{SHCOST(K_0, Y', Z_K)}{TCOST(K_0, Y', P_K)}$, which compares points A and D in Fig. 2.1. On the other hand, the average cost CU_C measure is given by $\frac{TCOST(Y')}{TCOST(Y^*)}$, which compares point B with point A in Fig. 2.1. The shadow cost measure is a direct representation of the primal CU_q since it depends upon the deviation between shadow cost and actual cost at Y'. On the other hand, the average cost measure represents realised cost of being at Y', given K_0, as compared to Y^* which is consistent with K_0.

According to Morrison (1985b, 1988c) both the cost CU measures (shadow and average) are useful characterisation of CU_C and contain the same information. Thus there is a unique cost CU measure. However, shadow-valuation CU_C is preferred because *(i)* it is easy to measure, *(ii)* it traces fluctuations in CU_q as it is dependent on the same information, that is, the difference between Z_K and P_K, and *(iii)* it is still valid with NCRTS (as we would see below).

In case of NCRTS (Fig. 2.2) the optimal production level is not the minimum point of the LRAC curve, rather the tangency between SRAC and LRAC. In this case an increase in output from optimum level y^* results in a decline in average cost because of scale economies. Hence such decline should be disentangled from the dis-equilibrium cost due to quasi-fixity[10]. Thus the average cost CU_C measure, which compares points A and B, is difficult to ascertain. However, the shadow cost $CU_{C'}$, which compares points A and D, is still relevant in case of NCRTS.

In (2.15) it was given that $CU_C = \frac{C^*}{C}$ where $C^* = VC + Z_K K$ is shadow total cost and $C = VC + P_K K$ is total cost realised so that

$$CU_C = \frac{C - P_K K + Z_K K}{C} = \frac{C - (P_K - Z_K)K}{C} = 1 - (P_K - Z_K)\frac{K}{C} \quad ...(2.21)$$

An implication of (2.21) is that whenever $P_K = Z_K$ there is full utilisation of capacity. In the case of $Z_K \neq P_K$ one can draw the same inference as in the case of CU_q described earlier.

A little re-arrangement of (2.21) reveals that[11]

$$CU_C = 1 - (P_K - Z_K)\frac{K}{C} = 1 - \frac{\partial C}{\partial K} \cdot \frac{K}{C} = 1 - \frac{\partial \ln C}{\partial \ln K} = 1 - \varepsilon_{CK} \quad ...(2.22)$$

where ε_{CK} is the elasticity of cost with respect to capital stock.

Equation (2.22) has an implication that when K adjusts to its equilibrium level in the long-run there is no tendency to change the capital stock and thus $\varepsilon_{CK} = 0$. Consequently, there is full utilisation of capacity in the long-run and the problem of over-utilisation or excess capacity is a short-run problem[12].

Estimation of Scale Economies

Long-run returns to scale (LRTS) has been estimated, within a PSE framework, by using an estimated variable cost function in a number of studies [see for example, Caves, Christensen and Swanson 1981; Friedleander and Spady 1981; Nelson 1985 among others]. For estimation of LRTS there are two different methods based on the variable cost function. One, the approach followed in Friedlander and Spady (1981) where the short-run cost function is first enveloped using the price of fixed factors in order to determine the long-run cost function. Two, the method used in Caves, Christensen and Swanson (1981), where LRTS is estimated directly from an estimated variable cost function. The difference between these measures boils down to the use of the level of capital stock at its actual level [Caves, Christensen and Swanson 1981] or equilibrium level [Friedlander and Spady 1981].

According to Brautigam and Daughety (1983) the choice between the two measures of LRTS should be based on the policy environment surrounding the industry. In the case of a regulatory regime with Averch-Johnson effect[13] it is likely that an industry has little incentive to adjust its capital stock to its equilibrium level. In such a case LRTS should be measured at the current level of K. However, if the capital stock approaches its equilibrium level within a reasonable period of time the Averch-Johnson effect is negligible and LRTS is measured at the equilibrium capital stock.

Results from earlier studies on scale economies in the Indian paper industry refer to production function of the Cobb-Douglas type and time-periods prior to the present one. In these studies empirical estimates of scale economies have not reached a consensus. While Sastry and Murty (1957) and Mehta (1976) argue that the Indian paper industry experienced constant returns to scale, Banerjee (1975) finds the presence of scale economies. With a more recent set of data and a translog cost function Pradhan and Barik (1999b) found the presence of diseconomies of scale in the paper industry for the period 1963-93. However, such a finding is derived from a FSE framework.

Estimation of Equilibrium Capital Stock

An essential element of the CU estimation is the estimation of equilibrium capital stock, K^*. Theoretically, the long-run total cost function is obtained from the short-run variable cost function by minimising total cost given variable cost function and the price of fixed input. Thus the industry is considered to have reached equilibrium if it does not feel the need of changing its capital stock unless there is a change in variable input prices or output. The optimisation problem under consideration is

$$\min_{K} G(Y,P_i,K,t)+P_K K \qquad ...(2.23)$$

In this formulation the equilibrium capital stock is given by equating the partial derivative of total cost with respect to capital to zero, that is, $\frac{\partial C}{\partial K}=0$. On application of this to (2.23) we obtain

$$\frac{\partial G}{\partial K}+P_K=0 \qquad ...(2.24)$$

As technology in the paper industry is characterised by a translog variable cost function (2.3) its logarithmic partial derivative with respect to K is given by

$$\frac{\partial \ln G}{\partial \ln K}=\beta_K+\beta_{KK}\ln K+\beta_{KL}\ln(P_L/P_M)+\beta_{KE}\ln(P_E/P_M)+\beta_{KY}\ln Y+\beta_{KT}t \qquad ...(2.25)$$

We can solve for (2.24) by substituting values from (2.25) so as to obtain the equilibrium capital stock K^* such that

$$\frac{VC}{K}(\beta_K+\beta_{KK}\ln K+\beta_{KL}\ln(P_L/P_M)+\beta_{KE}\ln(P_E/P_M)+\beta_{KY}\ln Y+\beta_{KT}t)+P_K=0 \qquad ...(2.26)$$

It is useful to mention that closed form solution of (2.26) is not possible as K enters in both absolute and logarithmic terms. Thus K^* is found out by numerical or iterative method at each observation[14].

Measurement of Returns to Scale

Returns to scale is defined as the proportionate increase in output resulting from a proportionate increase in all inputs such that

$$\eta^{-1}=\frac{d\ln Y}{d\ln X}$$

where η is the inverse of returns to scale, Y is output and X is the input vector. Thus returns to scale (η^{-1}) is measured from the production function. However, taking advantage of the duality theorem, η^{-1} can be estimated from the cost function. In such a procedure η is defined as proportionate increase in cost due to a proportionate increase in output and returns to scale is projected as its inverse. In equation form

$$\eta^{-1} = \frac{1}{\partial \ln C / \partial \ln Y} \quad ...(2.27)$$

where C is total cost. Thus η is the 'cost flexibility', such that

$$\eta = \frac{\partial \ln C}{\partial \ln Y} \quad ...(2.28)$$

In a partial static equilibrium (PSE) framework what we estimate empirically is a variable cost function, not the total cost one. Consequently, we need a measure of scale economies, which is different from the usual measure based on instantaneous adjustment of all the inputs as in (2.27).

Short-Run Scale Economies

In the short-run the industry is in a temporary equilibrium, which is likely to change. In such a situation scale economies reflects the returns to variable factors only, which is termed short-run returns to scale (SRTS). Here SRTS is the inverse of short-run cost flexibility given by

$$\varepsilon_{CY}^{SR} = \frac{\partial \ln VC}{\partial \ln Y} \quad ...(2.29)$$

By taking partial derivative of translog variable cost function with respect to output we obtain

$$\frac{\partial \ln VC}{\partial \ln Y} = \beta_Y + \beta_{YY} \ln Y + \beta_{LY} \ln(P_L/P_M) + \beta_{EY} \ln(P_E/P_M) + \beta_{YK} \ln K + \beta_{Yt} t \quad ...(2.30)$$

Estimation of ε_{CY}^{SR} from (2.30) is straightforward, given the parameters of the variable cost function, and SRTS is estimated by taking the inverse of ε_{CY}^{SR}.

Long-Run Scale Economies

A measure of long-run returns to scale (LRTS) is more

relevant as all factors are adjusted to their equilibrium levels and the industry is in full equilibrium. In a PSE framework LRTS is given by. [Braeutigam and Daughety 1983]

$$\eta^{-1} = \frac{1-\partial \ln VC/\partial \ln K}{\partial \ln VC/\partial \ln Y} \qquad \text{...(2.31)}$$

where K is at its equilibrium level K^*. For estimation of η^{-1} according to (2.31) we need to have values for $\frac{\partial \ln VC}{\partial \ln K}$ and $\frac{\partial \ln VC}{\partial \ln Y}$, of which the former is already obtained in (2.25). For the latter one, we take logarithmic differentiation of the short-run variable cost function and obtain

$$\frac{\partial \ln VC}{\partial \ln Y} = \beta_Y + \beta_{YY} \ln Y + \beta_{LY} \ln(P_L/P_M) + \beta_{EY} \ln(P_E/P_M) + \beta_{KY} \ln K + \beta_{Yt} t \qquad \text{...(2.32)}$$

By evaluating (2.31) at all data points we obtain an estimate of LRTS. It is worth mentioning that here K is taken at its equilibrium level.

Relationship between SRTS and LRTS

We bring out the relationship between SRTS and LRTS in a PSE framework. Morrison (1992) has shown that there is a unique relationship between SRTS and LRTS. Starting with a total cost function we observe that, change in total cost due to variation in output is given by two parts: response to variable inputs keeping capital as fixed and response to variations in capital. Thus

$$\frac{d \ln C}{d \ln Y} = \frac{dC}{dY} \cdot \frac{Y}{C} = \frac{Y}{C} \left(\left. \frac{\partial C}{\partial Y} \right|_{K=\bar{K}} + \frac{\partial C}{\partial K} \cdot \frac{dK}{dY} \right) \qquad \text{...(2.33)}$$

In mathematical notations (2.33) is represented by

$$\eta = \varepsilon_{CY} + \frac{\partial C}{\partial K} \cdot \frac{K}{C} \cdot \frac{dK}{dY} \cdot \frac{Y}{K} = \varepsilon_{CY} + \varepsilon_{CK} \cdot \eta_K$$

where $\eta_K = \frac{d\ln K}{d\ln Y}$ is the inverse of returns to capital input. The above can be rearranged as

$$\varepsilon_{CY} = \eta - \varepsilon_{CK} \cdot \eta_K = \eta(1 - \frac{\eta_K}{\eta}\varepsilon_{CK}) \qquad ...(2.34)$$

In (2.34) we observe that ε_{CY} is the cost flexibility in the short-run while η is that in the long-run. Moreover, when technology is homothetic we have $\eta_K = \eta$. Thus we have the relationship

$$\varepsilon_{CY}^{SR} = CU \cdot \varepsilon_{CY}^{LR} \qquad ...(2.35)$$

where $\varepsilon_{CY}^{LR} = \eta$, and from (2.22) *CU* is given by $(1 - \varepsilon_{CK})$. An implication of (2.35) is that LRTS is the product of SRTS and CU.

Measurement of Mark-Up

According to Nadiri and Nandi (1999) productivity growth is more than a supply-side phenomenon. Demand-side factors such as market structure also play an important role in determining productivity growth.

In traditional TFP analysis it is generally assumed that perfect competition prevails in the product market which may not be realistic. More often the industry may not operate at the minimum point of the average cost curve in the long run and traditional TFP estimates may not be correct. In the case of perfect competition the demand curve for a firm is horizontal implying infinite demand elasticity whereas monopolistic traits make it downward sloping. Along with this, there is a divergence between the average revenue (AR) and marginal revenue (MR) curves. Such divergence is crucially dependent upon the elasticity of demand for the product and needs to be ascertained in empirical analysis. Thus adjustments in TFP for mark-up over marginal cost are somewhat different from those of scale economies and capacity utilisation in the sense that they are demand side adjustments rather than a supply side adjustments [Morrison 1992].

Some studies [Nadiri and Kim 1996; Park and Kwon 1995; Morrison 1992] have reported the presence of substantial mark-up in manufacturing industries. In the case of Korean manufacturing industries Park and Kwon (1995) have found substantial bias in traditional measures of productivity growth due to the presence of mark-up. On the basis of a generalised Leontief (GL) cost function estimated by Bayesian techniques they found the overall mark-up in Korean manufacturing industries to be 60 per cent during 1966-89. Nadiri and Kim (1996) estimate the extent of mark-up in the US, Japan and Korean manufacturing industries on the basis of a translog cost function to be 17 per cent, 20 per cent and 30 per cent respectively during the period 1971-90. It is useful to note that Korean manufacturing industries are common to the studies by Nadiri and Kim (1996) and Park and Kwon (1995) although the studies obtain substantially different estimates of mark-up. Such difference could be ascribed to the differences in estimation procedure, functional form and underlying producer behaviour. While Park and Kwon (1995) take a GL cost function and estimate it by Bayesian technique for the period 1966-89, the study by Nadiri and Kim (1996) is based on a TL cost function for the period 1970-1990 and estimated by a non-linear maximum likelihood method. Secondly, Park and Kwon (1995) take capital as a quasi-fixed variable while Nadiri and Kim (1996) treat physical as well as R&D capital as quasi-fixed variables.

There are two approaches available in the literature to deal with the problem of market imperfection. The first approach is to obtain estimates of demand elasticities from other studies and incorporate them into the traditional growth accounting equation [Denny, Fuss and Waverman 1981, for example]. The second one is to include the inverse output demand equation in the system of equations while estimating the variable cost function [Morrison 1992; Nadiri and Kim 1996; Park and Kwon 1995] so that the demand elasticity is obtained from within the system of equations.

In order to incorporate imperfect competition into the product market we need specification of two distinct features. First, in imperfect competition the demand curve is no longer perfectly elastic, that is, a horizontal straight line. Second, the market equilibrium condition, i.e., marginal cost (MC) is equal to marginal revenue (MR), needs to be brought explicitly into the system.

Inverse Output Demand Equation

The inverse output demand equation determines the elasticity of the demand curve facing the industry. We specify it by taking price as a function of several variables. The variables included in the study[15] are:

(i) output of paper,
(ii) per capita net national product (NNP), and
(iii) change in tastes and preference of people towards reading.

As a result the inverse output demand function is formulated as:

$$\ln P_Y = \alpha_0 + \alpha_Y \ln Y + \alpha_R \ln PCI + \alpha_t t \qquad ...(2.36)$$

where P_Y is output price, Y is output level, PCI is per capita NNP in India, and t is time variable representing tastes and preference of people.

Market Equilibrium Condition

In a perfectly competitive market the firm is a price taker and equilibrium product price (P_Y) is equal to the minimum level of industry average cost (AC) curve. Here, price equals marginal cost, that is,

$$\frac{\partial C}{\partial Y} = \frac{\partial VC}{\partial Y} = P_Y$$

On multiplication of both sides of the above by $\frac{Y}{VC}$ we have $\frac{\partial \ln VC}{\partial \ln Y} = \frac{P_Y Y}{VC}$. Thus logarithmic differentiation of (2.3) with respect to Y gives the revenue share equation as follows:

$$\frac{\partial \ln VC}{\partial \ln Y} = \frac{P_Y Y}{VC} = \beta_Y + \beta_{YY} \ln Y + \sum_i \beta_{iY} \ln P_i + \beta_{KY} \ln K + \beta_{Yt} t \qquad ...(2.37)$$

When the market is not perfectly competitive and monopolistic elements are present, the firm enjoys market power. In this specification the demand curve is not perfectly elastic and $P \neq MR$. As a result the equilibrium price level may not be at the minimum point of AC. However, the equilibrium output is achieved by equating MR with MC. By taking the derivative of the total revenue (TR) equation

$$TR = P_Y Y$$

we obtain

$$MR = \frac{\partial TR}{\partial Y} = P_Y + Y\frac{\partial P_Y}{\partial Y}$$

On substitution of the above relationship into the price mark-up ratio ($\frac{P_Y}{MC}$) we have

$$\frac{P_Y}{MC} = \frac{P_Y}{P_Y + Y \cdot \partial P_Y / \partial Y} = \frac{P_Y}{P_Y(1 + Y/P_Y \cdot \partial P_Y / \partial Y)} = \frac{P_Y}{P_Y(1 + \partial \ln P_Y / \partial \ln Y)} \quad ...(2.38)$$

We know from the inverse output demand equation (2.36) that $\frac{\partial \ln P_Y}{\partial \ln Y} = \alpha_Y$. Thus (2.38) is modified as follows:

$$\frac{P_Y}{MC} = \frac{1}{1 + \alpha_Y} \quad ...(2.39)$$

It is useful to note that by using (2.39) we get an estimate of mark-up over marginal cost in the industry.

By multiplying both sides of (2.39) by $\frac{Y}{VC}$ and re-arranging it we get

$$\frac{PY}{VC} = \frac{MC}{1 + \alpha_Y} \frac{Y}{VC} = \frac{1}{1 + \alpha_Y} \frac{\partial \ln VC}{\partial \ln Y}$$

Thus, in the presence of imperfect competition the output share equation (2.37) needs to be modified as follows:

$$\frac{P_Y Y}{VC} = (1 + \alpha_Y)^{-1}(\beta_Y + \beta_{YY} \ln Y + \sum_i \beta_{ij} \ln P_i + \beta_{KY} \ln K + \beta_{Yt} t) \quad ...(2.40)$$

It is worth noting that the above revenue share equation (2.40) is non-linear in parameters. Hence empirical implementation of (2.40) would require a non-linear estimation procedure.

Measurement of Substitution Elasticities

The concept of elasticity of substitution, introduced by Joan Robinson, is defined as the derivative of 'the ratio of two input levels' with respect to 'the ratio of two input prices'. In mathematical terms it is given by

$$\sigma_{12} = \frac{d\ln(X_1/X_2)}{d\ln(P_2/P_1)} \qquad \text{...(2.41)}$$

where σ represents elasticity of substitution, X is level of input and P is price of X.

In (2.41) a larger value of σ_{12} implies greater ease of substitution between inputs *1* and *2*. Moreover, if $\sigma_{12} > 1$ (<1) the share of input *1* becomes larger (smaller) relative to input *2* as the price of input *1* becomes relatively cheaper [Kang and Brown 1981].

When there are more than two inputs, the definition of elasticity of substitution becomes complex as it involves various partial derivatives. Accordingly there can be more than one definition depending upon the underlying assumption about variations in inputs. However, the partial elasticity of substitution defined by Allen [Allen 1938] and further elaborated by Uzawa (1962) is the most widely used concept[16] [Kang and Brown 1981], which is used in the study. The Allen partial elasticity of substitution[17] (APES), which is derived from a cost function, is given by:

$$A_{ij} = \frac{C \cdot C_{ij}}{C_i \cdot C_j} \qquad \text{...(2.42)}$$

where A_{ij} denotes the APES between inputs *i* and *j*, and the subscripts *i* and *j* in *C* represent first and second partial derivatives of *C* with respect to input prices P_i and P_j . The APES is similar to [Field and Berndt 1981]

$$A_{ij} = \frac{\partial \ln X_i}{\partial \ln P_j} \cdot \frac{1}{S_i}\bigg|_{Y=\bar{Y}} \quad ...(2.43)$$

where S_i is the cost share of ith input.

In APES we assume Y and t to remain unchanged while varying input prices. In (2.42) when $i \neq j$, A_{ij} indicates cross-elasticity of substitution whereas in case of $i = j$ it represents own elasticity.

The APES given at (2.42) provides us with some idea on whether two inputs are substitutes or complements. By substituting Shephard's lemma $\frac{\partial C}{\partial P_i} = X_i$ into (2.42) we obtain

$$A_{ij} = \frac{C(\partial X_i / \partial P_j)}{X_i X_j} \quad ...(2.44)$$

In (2.43) the cross elasticities A_{ij} indicate which inputs are substitutes or complements to each other. Logically two inputs are substitutes if increase in price of one input increases the demand for the other input. As C, X_i and X_j are positive, a positive (negative) value of $\frac{\partial X_i}{\partial P_j}$ indicates that inputs i and j are substitutes (complements)[18].

In the PSE framework, there is a distinction in underlying producer behaviour between the short-run and long-run. In the short-run prime concern before the industry is minimisation of variable cost given the stock of quasi-fixed input, in the present case capital. On the other hand, capital stock is adjusted to its equilibrium level in the long-run. Thus substitution between variable inputs is possible even in the short-run while substitution between variable factors and capital takes place only in the long-run. Accordingly there are both short-run (or sub-equilibrium) and long-run (or full equilibrium) elasticities of substitution.

Short-run Elasticities of Substitution

The short-run elasticities of substitution are computed from the short-run variable cost function. The expression given for APES at (2.42) is modified such that [Brown and Christensen 1981]

$$A_{ij}^{SR} = \frac{G \cdot G_{ij}}{G_i \cdot G_j} \qquad ...(2.45)$$

where A_{ij}^{SR} represents the short-run APES between inputs *i* and *j*, *G* is the variable cost function, and subscripts *i* and *j* are partial derivatives of *G* with respect to input prices P_i and P_j.

By taking first and second order derivatives of the translog short-run variable cost function and substituting in (2.44) we are in a position to estimate short-run APES.

It is useful to note that the short-run elasticities of substitution are valid only for the level of capital at which it is evaluated. If there is a change in the level of *K*, the estimates of A_{ij}^{SR} and A_{ii}^{SR} are inappropriate. Moreover, A_{ij}^{SR} and A_{ii}^{SR} are estimated only for the variable factors, viz., *L*, *E* and *M*. In order to have an estimate of elasticity of substitution between *K* and other factors we need to compute long-run APES.

Long-run Elasticities of Substitution

For estimation of long-run APES between inputs *i* and *j*, A_{ij}^{LR}, on the basis of (2.42) we need to have values for C, C_i,C_j and C_{ij}. In order to obtain these values we follow the algorithm given by Brown and Christensen (1981).

Since total cost is the sum of variable and fixed costs we have

$$C = G(P_i, Y, K, t) + P_K K^*$$

where K^* is equilibrium level of capital and subscript *i* denotes variable inputs *L, E* and *M*. By taking partial derivative of the above, we have

$$C_i = \frac{\partial C}{\partial P_i} = \frac{\partial G}{\partial P_i} \qquad ...(2.46)$$

$$C_K = \frac{\partial C}{\partial P_K} = K^* \qquad ...(2.47)$$

$$C_{ij}=\frac{\partial^2 C}{\partial P_i \partial P_j}=\frac{\partial^2 G}{\partial P_i \partial P_j}+\frac{\partial^2 G}{\partial P_i \partial K}\cdot\frac{\partial K}{\partial P_j} \qquad ...(2.48)$$

$$C_{iK}=\frac{\partial^2 C}{\partial P_i \partial P_K}=\frac{\partial}{\partial P_i}\left(\frac{\partial C}{\partial P_K}\right)=\frac{\partial K}{\partial P_i} \qquad ...(2.49)$$

It is possible to derive all the partial derivatives required directly from the parameter estimates of the translog short-run variable cost function except for $\frac{\partial K}{\partial P_i}$. For a single quasi-fixed input Brown and Christensen (1981) derive this as

$$\frac{\partial K}{\partial P_i}=-\frac{\partial I_K/\partial P_i}{\partial I_K/\partial K} \qquad ...(2.50)$$

where $I_K=\frac{\partial C}{\partial K}$.

Taking into account the identity $C=G(P_i,Y,K,t)+P_K K^*$ we find that

$$I_K=\frac{\partial C}{\partial K}=\frac{\partial G}{\partial K}+P_K=\frac{VC}{K}\cdot\frac{\partial \ln G}{\partial \ln K}+P_K \qquad ...(2.51)$$

From (2.51) we are in a position to derive the required partial derivatives in (2.50) such that

$$\frac{\partial I_K}{\partial P_i}=\frac{VC}{K}\cdot\frac{1}{P_i}\cdot\frac{\partial^2 \ln G}{\partial \ln K\,\partial \ln P_i}=\frac{VC}{KP_i}\beta_{iK}, \text{ and}$$

$$\frac{\partial I_K}{\partial K}=\frac{VC}{K}\cdot\frac{1}{K}\cdot\frac{\partial^2 \ln G}{\partial \ln K^2}=\frac{VC}{K^2}\beta_{KK} \qquad ...(2.52)$$

In terms of the estimated cost function, the above equations are given as follows:

$$C_i = \frac{\partial G}{\partial P_i} = \frac{V\hat{C}}{P_i} \cdot \hat{S}_i \qquad ...(2.53)$$

where $V\hat{C}$ and $\hat{S}_i$ are estimated variable cost and i^{th} input share estimated at equilibrium level of K that is K^* respectively.

Similarly,

$$C_{ij} = \frac{V\hat{C}}{P_i P_j} \cdot (\hat{S}_i \hat{S}_j + \hat{\beta}_{ij}) \qquad ...(2.54)$$

$$C_{ii} = \frac{V\hat{C}}{P_i^2} \cdot (\hat{S}_i^2 - \hat{S}_i + \hat{\beta}_{ii}) \qquad ...(2.55)$$

$$C_{iK} = -\frac{\beta_{iK}\, V\hat{C}/K^* P_i}{\beta_{KK}\, V\hat{C}/K^{*2}} \qquad ...(2.56)$$

By substituting these values in (2.42) we find that

$$A_{ij}^{LR} = \frac{\hat{C} \cdot \frac{V\hat{C}}{P_i P_j}(\hat{S}_i \hat{S}_j + \hat{\beta}_{ij})}{\frac{V\hat{C}}{P_i} \cdot \hat{S}_i \frac{V\hat{C}}{P_j} \cdot \hat{S}_j} = \frac{\hat{C}}{V\hat{C}} \cdot \left(\frac{\hat{S}_i \hat{S}_j + \hat{\beta}_{ij}}{\hat{S}_i \hat{S}_j}\right) \qquad ...(2.57)$$

$$A_{ii}^{LR} = \frac{\hat{C} \cdot \frac{V\hat{C}}{P_i^2}(\hat{S}_i^2 - \hat{S}_i + \hat{\beta}_{ii})}{\frac{V\hat{C}}{P_i} \cdot \hat{S}_i \frac{V\hat{C}}{P_i} \cdot \hat{S}_i} = \frac{\hat{C}}{V\hat{C}} \cdot \left(\frac{\hat{S}_i^2 - \hat{S}_i + \hat{\beta}_{ii}}{\hat{S}_i^2}\right) \qquad ...(2.58)$$

and,

$$A_{iK}^{LR} = -\frac{\hat{C} \cdot \frac{\beta_{iK} K^*}{\beta_{KK} P_i}}{\frac{V\hat{C}}{P_i} \hat{S}_i \cdot K^*} = -\frac{\hat{C}}{V\hat{C}} \cdot \frac{\beta_{iK}}{\beta_{KK} \hat{S}_i} \qquad ...(2.59)$$

Once we have estimates of a variable cost function, we are in a position to obtain estimates of long-run APES in the industry.

Estimation of Price Elasticities

The price elasticity of demand (E_{ij}) for input *i* with respect to input *j* is defined as

$$E_{ij} = \frac{\partial \ln X_i}{\partial \ln P_j} \qquad ...(2.60)$$

where X_i is the level of the ith input and P_j is the price of the jth input. Following Field and Berndt (1981) we derive E_{ij} from the APES estimated earlier. According to Field and Berndt (1981) the APES is equivalent to the following:

$$A_{ij} = \frac{\partial \ln X_i}{\partial \ln P_j} \cdot \frac{1}{S_i}\bigg|_{Y=\bar{Y}} \qquad ...(2.61)$$

From (2.60) we derive the price elasticity of demand for input *i* with respect to input *j* as follows:

$$E_{ij} = \frac{\partial \ln X_i}{\partial \ln P_j} = S_i A_{ij} \qquad ...(2.62)$$

In our PSE framework the production characteristics are derived from the estimates of translog variable cost function. The estimation procedure of a translog variable cost function is given in the Chapter 3. Based on empirical data of the Indian paper industry we estimate CU, scale economies, mark-up and substitution elasticities which are presented in Chapter 4.

Notes

1. In Chapter 5 we discuss the salient features of PSE framework along with those of full static equilibrium and partial dynamic equilibrium.

2. The translog cost function is a dual to the translog production function [Christensen, Jorgenson and Lau 1971, 1973]. The translog production function is given as

$$\ln Y = \beta_0 + \sum_i \beta_i \ln X_i + \frac{1}{2}\sum_i \sum_j \beta_{ij} \ln X_i \ln X_j + \sum_i \beta_{it} \ln X_i t + \beta_t t + \frac{1}{2}\beta_{tt} t^2 \quad (i = K, L, E, M)$$

with the following restrictions: $\sum_i \beta_i = 1;\ \sum_i \beta_{ij} = \sum_j \beta_{ij} = \sum_i \beta_{it} = 0;\ \beta_{ij} = \beta_{ji}$

3. In general terms the short-run variable cost function is given by $VC = G(P_V, Y, K, t)$ where $VC = P_L L + P_E E + P_M M$ is the total variable cost of producing output Y with level of technology *t*.
4. We borrow the notations from Nadiri and Kim (1996).
5. Shephard (1953) has shown that under equilibrium conditions $\frac{\partial C}{\partial P_i} = X_i$, where X_i is the equilibrium level of the ith input. Thus $\frac{\partial \ln VC}{\partial \ln P_i} = \frac{\partial VC}{\partial P_i}\frac{P_i}{VC} = \frac{P_i X_i}{VC} = S_i$.
6. As technology is no more constrained to constant returns to scale, the revenue share (s_i) may not be equal to the cost share (S_i).
7. The method of derivation of K^* is discussed later in p. 23.
8. The shadow price of capital is its intrinsic price to the industry. Lau (1978) has shown that $Z_K = -\frac{\partial G}{\partial K}$, where $G(P_V, Y, K, t)$ is the variable cost function. Thus Z_K gives the decline in variable cost due to a unit increase in capital. Morrison (1986) defines it to be equal to Tobin's q.
9. In order to maintain linear homogeneity in input prices we normalise (2.3) by one of the variable input prices, which results in its modification. See (3.8) in Chapter 3.
10. In the case of the long-run CRTS such a problem does not arise, as LRAC is a horizontal straight line. Thus any deviation in average cost from LRAC can be ascribed to dis-equilibrium cost.
11. Since $C = G(\cdot) + P_K K$ we find that $\frac{\partial C}{\partial K} = \frac{\partial G}{\partial K} + P_K = -Z_K + P_K$.
12. When there is long-run CRTS, $CU_C = \varepsilon_{CY}$. By taking logarithmic total derivative of C we find $\frac{d \ln C}{d \ln Y} = \frac{\partial C}{\partial Y}\frac{Y}{C} + \frac{\partial C}{\partial K}\frac{dK}{dY}\frac{Y}{C} =$

$$\frac{\partial \ln C}{\partial \ln Y} + \frac{\partial \ln C}{\partial \ln K} = \varepsilon_{CY} + \varepsilon_{CK} = 1, \text{ since } \frac{dK}{dY} = \frac{K}{Y} \text{ with CRTS. Thus}$$

from (2.22) $CU_C = 1 - \varepsilon_{CK} = \varepsilon_{CY}$ [Morrison 1988a, 1988c].

13. The Averch-Johnson effect refers to the conclusion that if the allowed rate of return exceeds the actual cost of capital, then a profit maximising firm adopts more capital-intensive technology than warranted by its efficient expansion path [Averch and Johnson 1962].
14. Readymade software to solve for the equilibrium level of *K* numerically was not available to us. Thus a program was to be written using computer language FORTRAN.
15. There could be many other contending variables which appear to be influencing demand for paper and paper products, e.g., literacy rate, school enrolment, share of service sector in GDP, etc. However, inclusion of such variables did not improve the results and on estimation, the coefficients of these variables were found to be statistically not significant.
16. Other related concepts available in the literature are McFadden's direct elasticity of substitution and Morishima's full elasticity of substitution. See Kang and Brown (1981) for a discussion and empirical estimation of these concepts.
17. Some studies term it the Allen-Uzawa partial elasticity of substitution (AUPES) in due recognition of the contribution made by Uzawa (see, for example, Jorgenson 1986).
18. Further simplification of (2.43) in case of a translog cost function shows that $A_{ij} = \dfrac{\beta_{ij} + S_i S_j}{S_i S_j}$ and $A_{ii} = \dfrac{\beta_{ii} - S_i + S_i^2}{S_i^2}$ [Berndt and Wood 1975].

3

Towards Empirical Estimation

For empirical estimation of the production characteristics of the Indian paper industry discussed in the previous chapter we have two requirements: an estimation procedure and a database. These two aspects are covered in the present chapter.

It is worth recalling that we attempt to estimate the production characteristics such as capacity utilisation, scale economies, mark-up over marginal cost, and substitution elasticities. For this purpose we adopt a partial static equilibrium framework in the sense that capital is a quasi-fixed input while labour, energy and raw materials are variable inputs. Technology in the Indian paper industry is characterised by a translog variable cost function. As shown in the previous chapter it is possible to derive the production characteristics mentioned above from the parameters of the translog variable cost function. Thus the prime concern before us is the estimation of a translog variable cost function.

The Equation System and Estimation Procedure

The Equation System

As mentioned in the previous chapter, the translog variable cost function taken for estimation takes the following form:

$$\ln VC = \beta_0 + \beta_Y \ln Y + \sum_i \beta_i \ln P_i + \beta_K \ln K + \frac{1}{2}\beta_{YY}(\ln Y)^2 + \frac{1}{2}\sum_i \sum_j \beta_{ij} \ln P_i \ln P_j$$
$$+ \frac{1}{2}\beta_{KK}(\ln K)^2 + \sum_i \beta_{iY} \ln Y \ln P_i + \sum_i \beta_{ij} \ln K \ln P_i + \beta_{KY} \ln K \ln Y$$
$$+ \sum_i \beta_{it} \ln P_i t + \beta_{Yt} \ln Y t + \beta_t t + \frac{1}{2}\beta_{tt} t^2 + \beta_{Kt} \ln K\, t$$
$$(i, j = L, E, M) \qquad ...(3.1)$$

The cost function at (3.1) should be homogeneous of degree one in input prices. This requires imposition of the following restrictions on (3.1):

$$\sum_i \beta_i = 1; \;\; \sum_i \beta_{ij} = \sum_i \beta_{iy} = \sum_i \beta_{it} = \sum_i \beta_{ik} = 0; \;\; \beta_{ij} = \beta_{ji} \qquad ...(3.2)$$

The input demand function for (3.1) are represented by the factor share equations given as follows:

$$S_i = \beta_i + \sum_j \beta_{ij} \ln P_j + \beta_{iK} \ln K + \beta_{iY} \ln Y + \beta_{it} t \qquad ...(3.3)$$

There are three share equations, one for each variable input (*i* = *L, E, M*). In addition to the variable cost function and share equations we also have the inverse output demand equation

$$\ln P_Y = \alpha_0 + \alpha_Y \ln Y + \alpha_R \ln PCI + \alpha_t t \qquad ...(3.4)$$

and the revenue share equation

$$\frac{P_Y Y}{VC} = (1 + \alpha_Y)^{-1}(\beta_Y + \beta_{YY} \ln Y + \sum_i \beta_{ij} \ln P_i + \beta_{KY} \ln K + \beta_{Yt} t) \qquad ...(3.5)$$

We derive the share equations representing input demand functions from the variable cost function. Thus the disturbances in these share equations at a given time are likely to reflect some common unmeasurable or omitted factors and hence could be correlated. Existence of correlation between disturbances from different equations, known as contemporaneous correlation', may require joint estimation of all equations to gain efficiency. The appropriate joint estimation technique often used is seemingly unrelated regression estimation (SURE) [Judge *et al.* 1988].

Berndt and Wood (1975) have estimated the cost share equations as a multivariate regression equation system. This procedure, however, does not provide estimates for β_Y and β_{YY} apart from β_0 which do not appear in the share equations. Since Berndt and Wood (1975) assume constant returns to scale (CRTS) as a maintained hypothesis, the cost share equations included all the parameters (except β_0) in their case[1]. Thus, in cases where CRTS is not assumed estimation of cost or revenue shares alone does not provide estimates for all relevant parameters.

We follow the practice of Christensen and Greene (1976) who estimate the translog cost function together with the cost share equations. By doing so we would be gaining in efficiency as the degrees of freedom increase while the number of parameters remains the same. Due to such an advantage, we presume, it has been accepted as a common practice [see Berndt and Hesse 1986; Caves *et al.* 1981; Nadiri and Kim 1996 among others].

Error Covariance Structure

We need to add an error term to the cost function (3.1) in empirical estimation because of its stochastic nature[2]. As the cost share equations at (3.2) are derived from the translog cost function by logarithmic differentiation, they do not contain a disturbance term from the cost function. We follow Berndt and Wood (1975) and assume that deviations of the cost share equations from logarithmic derivatives of the translog cost function are the result of random errors in cost minimising behaviour. Thus we append an additive disturbance term to each share equation.

Since the factor shares sum to unity, one of the share equations is redundant. Moreover, the error terms included in the share equations are contemporaneous and sum to zero. This makes the error covariance matrix singular and estimation is not feasible if all share equations are included in the system. Following Berndt and Wood (1975) we drop one of the share equations[3] so that the error covariance matrix is non-singular and estimation is feasible.

There are 5 equations in the system to be estimated jointly. The error terms added to the equations are assumed to be jointly normally distributed. In the system input prices and technology are assumed to be exogenously given[4].

In ideal situations the error terms in the equations are not autocorrelated and have a constant variance within each equation. However, in empirical analysis they may be autocorrelated and may not have identical variance. The twin problems, autocorrelation and heteroskedasticity, have to be taken into account while estimating the equations. Generally it is seen that time series data exhibit a problem of autocorrelation while heteroskedasticity is more likely to be present in cross-section data [Judge et al. 1988]. Since the present study deals with time series data we need to look into possible autocorrelation among error terms[5]. Autocorrelation can arise because of any excluded variable, incorrect functional specification or manipulation of data.

We rule out the possibility of serial correlation between error terms across equations. However, autocorrelation between error terms in the same equation is taken into account. In particular, we assume that error terms follow a first order autoregressive (AR1)[6] process given as follows:

$$u_t = \rho u_{t-1} + v_t \qquad ...(3.6)$$

where u_t is the error in an equation for the period t,

v_t is the error term which is identically independently distributed with zero mean and constant variance, and

ρ is the first order autocorrelation coefficient.

In (3.6) the data generating process is stationary if $|\rho| < 1$. A stationary process as defined here and in most of the empirical studies, implies that the mean, variance and covariances of u_t do not change over time[7]. For a first order stationary process, by recursive substitution, it is possible to show that

$$u_t = v_t + \rho v_{t-1} + \rho^2 v_{t-2} + ... = \sum_{i=0}^{\infty} \rho^i v_{t-i} \qquad ...(3.7)$$

An implication of (3.7) is that the error term u_t can be expressed as a weighted sum of a time series of uncorrelated and identically distributed random errors $v_t, v_{t-1}, v_{t-2}, \ldots$ with the weights $1, \rho, \rho^2, \ldots$. These weights decline geometrically if $|\rho| < 1$ [Judge et al. 1988]. In order to simplify the estimation process we assume the value of ρ to be the same for all the equations[8].

Estimation Method

The cost function specified at (3.1) fulfils the conditions of linear homogeneity in prices if the conditions specified at (3.2) are met. Thus at the estimation stage these restrictions need to be imposed on the cost function. An alternative to this, however, is to normalise the variable input prices. As a result, the restricted cost function satisfies the conditions of linear homogeneity in input prices and no additional restriction needs to be imposed at the estimation stage [Nadiri and Kim 1996]. The present study normalises P_L and P_E by P_M. Such a modification results in the following functional form for (3.1):

$$\begin{aligned}\ln VC = {} & \beta_0 + \ln P_M + \beta_L \ln(P_L/P_M) + \beta_E \ln(P_E/P_M) + \beta_Y \ln Y + \beta_K \ln K + \frac{1}{2}\beta_{YY}(\ln Y)^2 \\ & + \frac{1}{2}\beta_{LL}\ln(P_L/P_M)^2 + \frac{1}{2}\beta_{EE}\ln(P_E/P_M)^2 + \beta_{LE}\ln(P_L/P_M)\ln(P_E/P_M) \\ & + \frac{1}{2}\beta_{KK}(\ln K)^2 + \beta_{LY}\ln(P_L/P_M)\ln Y + \beta_{EY}\ln(P_E/P_M)\ln Y + \beta_{KY}\ln K \ln Y \\ & + \beta_{Lt}\ln(P_L/P_M)_t\, t + \beta_{Et}\ln(P_E/P_M)t + \beta_{Yt}\ln Y\, t + \beta_t t + \frac{1}{2}\beta_{tt}t^2 + \beta_{Kt}\ln K\, t \\ & + \beta_{KL}\ln K \ln(P_L/P_M) + \beta_{KE}\ln K \ln(P_E/P_M) \qquad \ldots(3.8)\end{aligned}$$

Consequently the share equations are modified as follows:

$$S_L = \beta_L + \beta_{LL}\ln(P_L/P_M) + \beta_{LE}\ln(P_E/P_M) + \beta_{LK}\ln K + \beta_{LY}\ln Y + \beta_{Lt}t \quad \ldots(3.9)$$

$$S_E = \beta_E + \beta_{LE}\ln(P_L/P_M) + \beta_{EE}\ln(P_E/P_M) + \beta_{EK}\ln K + \beta_{EY}\ln Y + \beta_{Et}t \quad \ldots(3.10)$$

$$S_M = 1 - S_L - S_E \quad \ldots(3.11)$$

In addition, the output share equation, which is derived from (3.4) is modified as follows:

$$\frac{P_Y Y}{VC} = (1+\alpha_Y)^{-1}(\beta_Y + \beta_{YY}\ln Y + \beta_{LY}\ln(P_L/P_M) + \beta_{EY}\ln(P_E/P_M) + \beta_{KY}\ln K + \beta_{Yt}t) \ldots(3.12)$$

It can be seen from equations (3.9) to (3.11) that the share equations are homogeneous of degree zero. An implication of this is that equilibrium input requirements and output level do not change if there is a proportional change in input prices. However, the equilibrium levels of inputs and output change if there is a change in relative prices.

Thus we have a system of 5 equations comprising the variable cost function (3.8), two share equations[9] (3.9 and 3.10), the output share equation (3.12) and the inverse output demand equation (3.4) which need to be estimated jointly. We need a method of estimation different from seemingly unrelated regression (SUR) and suitable for estimation of a system of equations with contemporaneous correlation. This is because of two problems: One, the output variable is not exogenous as the output share equation (3.12) derived from the equilibrium condition is included in the system. Two, equation (3.12) is not linear in parameters. Following Nadiri and Kim (1996) we adopt the non-linear maximum likelihood method. The software package SHAZAM (White et al. 1997) is used for estimation of the equation system.

Data Sources

There are four inputs considered in the study of which three are variable (labour, energy and materials) while the remaining one is quasi-fixed (capital). Empirical estimation of such a model requires data on levels of cost, output and inputs as well as prices of inputs, which we take from the Annual Survey of Industries[10] (ASI) [Government of India (a)] conducted by the National Sample Survey (NSS) organisation and processed by the Central Statistical Organisation (CSO). However, the variables required for the study are not available directly from this source. This is mainly because of two reasons: one, the information contained in it are in value terms at historical prices; two, some of the information contained are for taxation purposes which poorly represent true variables. In order to circumvent the problem appropriate variables need to be constructed from the available statistics.

Keeping data availability and consistency in view we take the period 1973-74 to 1997-98. The paper industry at aggregate level is considered in the study and factories registered under sections 2m(i) and 2m(ii) of the Factories Act, 1948 are included. Data are taken for the 'factory sector' from the Annual Survey of Industries (ASI) [Government of India (a)]. It is useful to note that the factory sector includes factories employing 10 or more workers working with the aid of power (20 or more workers working without the aid of power).

The ASI data are available from 1959 onwards except for 1972-73 when the survey was not conducted. However, up to the year 1971-72 industrial classification in the ASI was according to the Standard Industrial Classification (SIC) for the census sector and the Labour Bureau Industrial Classification for the sample sector [Government of India 1999]. Synchronisation of both the sectors came with the National Industrial Classification[11] (NIC) 1970, results according to which are available since 1973-74. Till such time as the present study was drafted, ASI data were available up to the year 1997-98. Therefore, the study has taken the period 1973-74 to 1997-98 for analytical purposes[12].

A choice before us is between firm level data and aggregate industry level data. For the purpose of the present study our preference for aggregate data over firm level data is influenced by the following reasons:

(i) The paper industry comprises many firms each providing a negligible part of the industry output. According to CMIE the largest firm (Ballarpur Industries) produced only 6.47 per cent whereas the second largest firm (Hindustan Paper Corporation) produced 3.13 per cent of total output during 1997-98. The Herfindahl index[13] of concentration for the industry during 1997-98 is found to be 0.01 which implies that concentration in the industry is almost nil [CMIE 1999]. In such a situation policy inferences drawn on the basis of a limited number of firms is not likely to be representative enough for the industry.

(ii) Data at the firm level from secondary sources such as CMIE and RBI are available only for a small number of firms and for a limited number of years. Moreover, data for many firms are not available on a continuous basis. Hence, a consistent and sufficiently long data set could

not be obtained for econometric estimation of a cost function envisaged in the study.

(iii) Firm level data available from CMIE and RBI sources in fact do not pertain to plant level operations. A firm may go for horizontal combination of a number of small-sized plants to produce a higher level of output. As a result, important characteristics of production structure (particularly, scale economies, which show the effect of size on efficiency) do not get reflected properly even if firm level data are used.

(iv) A cost function, which is estimated for the Indian paper industry, requires data on input prices apart from data on cost and output. However, data at the firm level on input prices are not available. This makes the formulation of a cost function difficult.

The aggregate data at the three-digit level of ASI is taken into account. Particularly, industry groups bearing National Industrial Classification (NIC) 1970 codes 280, 281, 282 and 283 are included[14]. For the purpose of empirical estimation we take the total of the above four industry groups.

Further disaggregation, though possible from the ASI data, is not attempted because of the following reason: According to the ASI classification a factory producing more than one product is put in a particular category on the basis of the value of the principal product manufactured by it. Thus a production unit gets classified to only one industry group, that of the principal product. However, a change in the output mix in the subsequent year may put the factory in a different category. Firms in the paper industry produce a number of products in different combinations and there is a fair chance that a combination may change from time to time[15]. Thus taking data at a highly disaggregated level would result in measurement error and yearly fluctuations.

Estimation of Capital Stock

The measurement of capital input poses problems mainly because of two characteristics associated with it, namely, durability and heterogeneity. Capital stock, unlike other inputs, has the basic feature that once built, it does not get fully exhausted in a single use; rather it stays for a longer period. Thus what it provides to the production process are its services. Secondly, capital goods are extremely heterogeneous and thus cannot be aggregated in physical terms. We have to look into capital goods in value terms so as to obtain an aggregate value.

The process of embodiment in capital of initial investment and the services provided by capital as a factor of production spanning over time are contentious issues[16]. The importance of a realistic capital stock estimate can be assessed from the fact that substantial differences in results for the same period and industry can be ascribed to the differences in capital stock estimation [Goldar 1986]. This brings forth the following features of capital input:

- As mentioned earlier, capital input provides capital services to the production process. Thus what we need to measure is the quantity of capital services rather than its stock. In full static equilibrium models with instantaneous adjustment, it is generally assumed that the quantity of capital services is proportional to the level of capital stock [Jorgenson and Griliches 1967]. In cases where there is excess capacity or over-utilisation of capital stock such proportionality does not hold.
- Second, unlike labour and intermediate inputs, a perfect market for capital goods does not exist. This is so because the consumer of capital, in general, is its supplier also [Jorgenson and Griliches 1967]. Part of capital inputs in the production process may be hired but mostly it is owned by the producer. Thus in the absence of market place transactions we rely on imputed values for the price of capital services.
- Third, an important feature of capital input is that while being used in the production process, it does not remain intact due to wear and tear, that is, depreciation. The rate and pattern of depreciation applicable to capital stock has to be determined before we reach a realistic estimate of capital stock.
- Fourth, along with depreciation of initial capital stock there may be a decline in efficiency and ultimate retirement of existing capital stock. The decline in efficiency over

time poses a further problem in aggregating capital of different vintages. Capital stock of different vintages and, therefore, the services provided by them need not be of the same efficiency. Hence, combining such heterogeneous capital stocks and finding an aggregate figure at any point of time is difficult.

The present study assumes technological change to be 'disembodied' in the sense that capital stock of different vintages differ only by some fixed factor associated with depreciation and retirement of capital. Thus if there is technological progress through process innovation[17] then new processes make use of existing capital and labour to produce more of the same product. The rate of depreciation (δ) converts each vintage of investment into new-machine equivalents. Consequently the stock of capital at time t, K_t, can be interpreted as the number of new-machine equivalents implied by past investments [Hulten 1992]. Thus an investment, once made, to build capital stock will provide its services to the production process till retirement, *albeit* at an ever-reducing rate.

In empirical measurement from published data, capital stock estimates generally are derived from book values by the perpetual inventory method[18]. It involves adding capital formation to an initial capital stock (the benchmark capital) and subtracting capital assets that are withdrawn from the stock. In this method four types of information are required: *(i)* benchmark capital stock, *(ii)* annual capital formation or investment, *(iii)* the length of time that the asset remains in use (asset life), and *(iv)* changes in the price of capital services [Blades 1991].

We discuss below each of these issues keeping data sources discussed in the previous section in view.

Benchmark Capital Stock

Obtaining a realistic estimate of initial capital stock is quite important for a study of the present nature. Thus we should define unambiguously what constitutes capital. Generally, capital stock comprises *(i)* plant and machinery, *(ii)* land, *(iii)* buildings and construction, and *(iv)* other equipment (such as vehicles, etc.). In the context of our major data source, we note that the ASI provides data on book value of fixed capital on a yearly basis. This book value represents the depreciated values of fixed assets owned by the factory on the closing day of the accounting year. Fixed assets are defined as those which have a normal productive life of more than one year [Government of India (a)]. Thus it excludes intangible assets and assets solely used for post-manufacturing activities such as sale, storage, distribution, etc.

The book value figures as a measure of capital stock suffer from two major problems: *(i)* these figures are written down (depreciated) book values, not the original purchase price of the assets, and *(ii)* they are aggregations of annual additions made in the past, each addition being at different prices [Hasim and Dadi 1973]. Depreciation, which is used to reach book values in the ASI, is at rates allowed by tax officials and does not represent true wear and tear due to production. Thus a book value figure is not an appropriate measure of capital input [Banerjee 1975].

However, gross capital stock can be derived from book values. In a distinguished study Hashim and Dadi (1973) estimate gross capital stock for the year 1960 from book values by studying the balance sheets of 1000 firms. Analysing these at the 3-digit industrial classification level, they estimate the gross-net ratio (GNR) for individual industries. Using this GNR, book values can be converted to gross capital stock at purchase price for the year 1960. The GNR for the paper industry for different components of capital are reproduced[19] from Hashim and Dadi (1973) in Table 3.1.

Table 3.1
Gross-Net Ratio for Paper Industry

Capital	*GNR*
Building and Construction	1.4501
Plant and Machinery	1.6906
Other Equipment	1.8135
Land	1.0000

Note: Hashim and Dadi (1973) exclude land from fixed capital.
Source: Hashim and Dadi (1973), Table III.1.

By applying the GNR given in Table 3.1 to the book values of fixed capital, component-wise, for the year 1960 we obtain the gross capital stock at purchase price for the year 1960 at current prices. According to Hashim and Dadi (1973) gross value or purchase price of capital is the closest concept to capital in theory.

A contentious issue in productivity studies based on ASI data is what constitutes capital. While taking book values Hashim and Dadi (1973) exclude value of land and cash in hand[20]. The value of land is not included on the ground that it does not have an important role in manufacturing sector. However, they include the value of improvements on land in the form of building and construction. Cash is excluded from the definition of capital as real goods alone can form capital when used in the production process. Cash only represents a claim against real goods and in aggregate such claims cancel out.

The standard practice in productivity studies on Indian manufacturing industries has been along the following lines: first to take the book value of fixed capital including land to derive the benchmark capital stock [Ahluwalia 1985 & 1991; Banerjee 1975; Goldar 1986; Balakrishnan and Pushpangadan 1994 among others]; second to exclude working capital from the definition of capital[21]. The present study proceeds along these lines.

Capital Formation

The stock of capital adjusts to its equilibrium level through investment. Investment is the addition to capital stock over a period of time, usually a year in case of annual data. A problem with the ASI data is that it does not contain any entry on investment. However, the difference between book value of fixed capital for successive years provides an estimate of net investment [Hashim and Dadi 1973]. Adding depreciation values provided in the ASI to such investment figures we obtain gross investment, I_t, at current prices. Thus,

$$I_t = (F_t - F_{t-1}) + D_t \quad ...(3.13)$$

where F_t is the book value of fixed capital for year t and D_t is the depreciation for year t.

Given the fact that book values of fixed capital are at historical prices, investment derived in (3.13) is at current prices. In order to have an approximation to the real value of investment these figures need to be converted into constant prices by means of appropriate index numbers.

Value of investment obtained in (3.13) is a composite figure comprising components of capital stock such as plant and machinery, land, buildings and construction, and other equipment (vehicles, etc.). Ideally we should have separate estimates of investment for these components and each component should be deflated by its price index. However, we do not have accurate investment figures in each segment because depreciation, which is added to net investment, is available only on an aggregate basis, not asset-wise.

As a deflator of investment goods, some of the studies [Banerjee 1975; Goldar 1986] have taken a weighted average of wholesale price indexes (WPI) of construction and machinery [Government of India (b)], the weights being base year proportion of machinery and buildings in the capital stock. Some of the studies based on firm level data also have followed this approach [Bharadwaj 1994; Panda 1998; Srivastava 1996]. Most of the studies in the area have avoided taking such an approach [for example, Ahluwalia 1985, 1991; Balakrishnan and Pushpangadan 1994; Basant and Fikkert 1996; Dholakia and Dholakia 1994; Gangopadhyay and Wadhwa 1998; Mitra 1999; Pradhan and Barik 1998, 1999a,b,c] and have used the WPI for machinery only. In line with these studies we deflated gross investment by the WPI of non-electrical machinery (average fiscal year) to the base 1981-82 [Chandhok 1990; Government of India (b)]. The choice of non-electrical machinery is on the basis of the fact that electrical machinery does not form a substantial part of total machinery in the paper industry.

Once the benchmark capital stock (K_0) for the year 1960 is given, the gross capital stock for year *t*, K_t, can be obtained by adding the sum of investments over the preceding years to K_0. As we have the series of investments in 1981-82 prices the benchmark capital stock also is inflated to 1981-82 prices.

In the present study we construct the capital stock series K_t (at constant price) by successive addition of gross investment at constant price. The following illustration will give a clearer picture of the procedure adopted. We take the gross capital stock for year t as

$$K_1 = K_0 + I_1$$

$$K_2 = K_1 + I_2 = K_0 + I_1 + I_2$$

....

$$K_t = K_{t-1} + I_t = K_0 + \sum_{i=0}^{t} I_{t-i} \qquad ...(3.14)$$

Here K_0 and I_t are in constant 1981-82 prices.

Asset Lives and Mortality Function

In the discussion so far we have obtained a time series of the gross capital stock. The shortcoming with the use of gross capital stock is that it does not provide for its wear and tear in the production process. An implication of this is that capital, once built, remains for all time to come and services provided by it do not decline over time. However, in practice, capital does get affected by obsolescence and is discarded.

It is quite a debatable issue whether we should use gross or net capital stock in the estimation of a cost function. Use of gross capital in the case of Indian manufacturing industries is suggested on the ground that a large part of current expenditure is incurred to maintain existing capital stock against wear and tear. Such expenditure is in the nature of replacement investment so that the productive capacity of capital remains intact. As a result the efficiency of the asset is maintained whereas the expenditures which should form part of depreciation do not get included. Thus further subtraction for depreciation is not warranted [Hashim and Dadi 1973]. Some of the studies such as Ahluwalia (1985 & 1991), Balakrishnan and Pushpangadan (1994), Banerjee (1975), Gangopadhyaya and Wadhwa (1998), Jha, Murty and Paul (1991), Jha, Murty, Paul and Rao (1993), Pradhan and Barik (1998, 1999a, 1999b) and Rao (1996), among others, do not provide for any depreciation in capital stock.

Such a view as above, however, ignores the efficiency decline due to obsolescence of capital. It is well known that new capital exhibits better efficiency than older capital. Secondly, if maintenance expenditure are not up to the requisite level for natural wear and tear of capital there is a decline in efficiency of capital[22]. Thirdly, capital stock gets discarded over time which is not reflected in gross capital stock. According to Goldar (1986) if capital discarding were not allowed the capital stock estimate would have an upward bias[23]. Keeping these points in view some of the studies have provided for depreciation of capital.

Depending upon the rate of depreciation and obsolescence, existing capital stock remains in use for a certain time period called 'asset life', which is influenced by the rate of decline in efficiency and ultimate disposal of capital. The retirement of capital is given by a mortality function, which can take many forms. Blades (1991) divided these mortality functions into three categories: *(i)* linear and delayed-linear, *(ii)* bell-shape, and *(iii)* simultaneous exit. In the linear retirement pattern assets are assumed to be discarded at the same rate (constant exponential decay) each year from the time of installation. In delayed-linear retirement starts after some time and is completed sooner than the linear case. With a bell shaped mortality function, the functional form assumed is generally log-normal, gamma, logistic, Weibull or Winfrey. In the case of simultaneous exit, all assets are retired from capital stock at the moment they reach the average service life[24]. Among these the exponential decay is by far the most widely used deterioration specification owing to its simplicity [Berndt 1991].

The asset lives are determined by expert advice, other country experience, surveys, etc. [Blades 1991]. As can be seen from Table 3.2, asset life for machinery in OECD countries varies from 12 years in Japan to 30 years in Sweden, with an arithmetic mean of 20 years.

A major problem with respect to use of any particular mortality function is that empirical evidence is scarce. Thus taking a particular functional form has its own arbitrariness. However, the constant exponential decay is simple to implement and finds some empirical support from a different strand of literature. In dynamic equilibrium models it is possible to estimate depreciation endogenously [Epstein and Danny 1980;

Prucha and Nadiri 1996]. These models allow for estimation of a rate of depreciation which varies over the sample. For example, according to Epstein and Danny (1980) the depreciation rate in the U.S. aggregate manufacturing sector varies from 0.11 to 0.145 with a mean of 0.126. However, some of these dynamic models could not reject a constant rate of depreciation [for example, Prucha and Nadiri 1996]. Thus assuming a constant rate of depreciation, which corresponds to constant exponential decay, is quite appealing.

Table 3.2
Average Service Lives of Machinery and Equipment in OECD Countries

	Country	*Service Life in Years*
1.	Australia	19
2.	Austria	18
3.	Belgium	15
4.	Canada	22
5.	Finland	17
6.	France	21
7.	Germany	16
8.	Iceland	22
9.	Italy	16
10.	Japan	12
11.	Norway	25
12.	Sweden	30
13.	United Kingdom	32
14.	United States	16
	Arithmetic Mean	20

Source: Blades (1991)

Indian productivity studies have not reached a mutually agreed upon asset life of capital stock and rate of depreciation. Some of the studies [Basant and Fikkert 1994; Bharadwaj 1994; Panda 1998] have assumed asset lives for capital assets in Indian manufacturing industries. Bharadwaj (1994) and Panda (1998) assume separate asset lives for *(i)* land and buildings, and *(ii)* plant and machinery. Bharadwaj (1994) takes the asset life of land and buildings to be 40 years while that of plant and machinery is taken to be 25 years in the case of the Indian iron and steel industry. On the other hand, Panda (1998) takes the asset life of land and buildings to be 50 years and that of plant and machinery to be 15 years in the case of the Indian road transport vehicle industry. However, such division of capital stock is not pursued in some of the studies which allow for capital depreciation [see for example, Basant and Fikkert 1994, Hulten and Srinivasan 1999, Majumdar 1996]. In a study where capital stock is not separated into its different types, Basant and Fikkert (1994) take the asset life of aggregate capital stock to be 16 years.

In the context of capital depreciation, Goldar (1986) uses gross capital instead of net capital but provides for capital discarding at the rate of 2 percent per annum[25]. Majumdar (1996) while undertaking a data envelopment analysis (DEA) of the Indian aggregate manufacturing sector provides for 10 percent per annum depreciation in capital stock. Goldar (1992) cites two studies [Antony 1962; Chaturvedi and Bagchi 1984] which have estimated the rate of discarding for Indian industries and have come out with linear discarding rate of 2.3 per cent and 3.3 per cent per annum respectively. While Basant and Fikkert (1996) assume that the full depreciation of capital takes 16 years at a rate of 6 per cent per annum, Hulten and Srinivasan (1999) apply 4 per cent annual depreciation.

The present study follows the practice of Hulten and Srinivasan (1999) and assumes 4 per cent depreciation on capital stock. As a result the average asset life of capital turns out to be about 25 years. Such an assumption is a little higher than the average in OECD countries but given the fact that capital is retained for a longer time span in India than in OECD countries, the presumption does not seem to be out of place.

The estimation of capital stock by the perpetual inventory method has to accommodate the desired depreciation rate, δ. Accordingly (3.13) is modified as follows:

$$K_1 = I_1 + (1-\delta)K_0$$

$$K_2 = I_2 + (1-\delta)K_1 = I_2 + (1-\delta)I_1 + (1-\delta)^2 K_0$$

....

$$K_t = I_t + (1-\delta)K_{t-1} \qquad ...(3.15)$$

We use K_t obtained from (3.14) as the capital input in the estimation of the translog short-run variable cost function discussed in the previous chapter.

Price of Capital Services

As mentioned earlier, we have to find out the price of capital services, which can be either at market rates or at shadow prices. The price of capital at shadow prices, defined as the 'real rate of return' to capital assets concerned, is difficult to estimate. Thus market rental of capital is used as a proxy for price of capital. However, this approach to price of capital also has its problems, which were discussed in the beginning of this section. To recapitulate, the one period user cost of capital is not observed directly. For some segments of capital, e.g., vehicles, rental price can be easily observed but it is not applicable to most of the capital input. This is because of non-availability of a perfectly competitive second hand capital market so that a firm is indifferent between renting and owning capital [Berndt 1991]. In such a situation the rental price of capital would equal the user cost. However, we have to resort to indirect methods of estimating price of capital services as capital is mostly owned and consumed by the firm itself.

According to Hall and Jorgenson (1967) the price of capital services (P_{Kt}) should comprise four components. First, the opportunity cost of having capital tied up with the present plant and equipment. Thus, if the price of investment goods is q_t and the current interest rate is r_t then opportunity cost is $q_t r_t$. Second, assuming that capital decays at a constant rate of δ the renter should compensate $q_t \delta$ to the owner. Third, since the capital good is durable it may undergo capital gains or losses. Hence the renter should compensate for expected price changes in capital goods, which amounts to Δq_t. Finally, there may be changes in direct taxes paid while purchasing the capital good. So the price of capital services should include expected changes in direct taxes also.

Jorgenson and Griliches (1967) suggest that in the absence of direct taxation the price of capital services should comprise the first three components. Thus

$$P_{Kt} = q_t(r_t + \delta - \frac{\Delta q_t}{q_t}) \qquad ...(3.16)$$

To simplify further, some studies while estimating translog cost function for Indian manufacturing industries, have taken the price of capital services to be the sum of the first two components [see, for example, Bharadwaj 1994; Jha and Sahni 1991; Jha, Murty and Paul 1994; Panda 1998] assuming that capital gains factors are absent. Following this practice, we define the price of capital services as follows:

$$P_{Kt} = q_t(r_t + \delta) \qquad ...(3.17)$$

We take WPI of non-electrical machinery and machine tools as the price of investment goods in paper industry. The rate of interest is taken to be the long term lending rate by banks such as IFCI and IDBI.

Construction of Other Variables

In addition to capital input, which is assumed to be quasi-fixed, there are three variable inputs included in the cost function defined in the study. These inputs are labour, energy and non-energy raw materials. We discuss below the procedure of constructing these variables.

Labour

The study takes 'total persons engaged[26]' by the factory as a measure of the labour variable. It may be noted that the ASI provides figures on five variables related to labour. These are *(i)* number of workers, *(ii)* mandays-workers, *(iii)* number of employees, *(iv)* mandays-employees and *(v)* total persons engaged. The category 'workers' is defined to include all persons employed, directly or through any agency, for wages or not, in the manufacturing process. It also includes labour engaged in repair or maintenance of fixed assets. However, it does not include persons holding positions of supervision or management, or employed in sales and purchase.

The category 'employees' includes, besides workers, persons receiving wages and holding managerial positions or supervisory staff in addition to persons engaged in sale, purchase and administration. The category 'total persons engaged' relates to all persons engaged whether for wages or not, in work connected directly or indirectly with the manufacturing process and includes all administrative, technical, clerical staff and also labour engaged in production of capital assets for a factory's own use. It also includes persons holding supervisory and managerial positions or engaged in administrative office, store keeping and welfare sections, sales and purchases departments and production of fixed assets for a factory's own use. Thus 'total persons engaged' describes better all labour input that has gone into the production process than the categories workers and employees. Hence it has been preferred in some of the important productivity studies on Indian manufacturing industries [see, for example, Ahluwalia 1985 and 1991; Balakrishnan and Pushpangadan 1994; Banerjee 1975; Goldar 1986; Pradhan and Barik 1998 among others].

The reward to labour is taken to be 'total emoluments' provided to employees, which is the total of wages and imputed value of benefits in kind. The average wage rate, which is taken as the price of labour input, is defined to be the ratio of emoluments to total persons engaged. The share of labour in output (variable cost) is 'total emoluments' divided by output (variable cost) at current prices.

Energy

Energy includes total purchase value, exclusive of taxes, of all items of fuel, lubricants, electricity, water and gasoline consumed by the factory during the accounting year. In addition to the above, gasoline and other fuels for vehicles, except those entering directly into products as materials consumed, are also included in energy. The price of energy is taken to be the WPI of fuel and lubricants. Energy's share in output (variable cost) is obtained by dividing value of fuels and lubricants as given in the ASI by output (variable cost) at current prices.

Materials

This component represents the total delivered value, exclusive of taxes, of all items of raw materials, components and chemicals which entered into the production process. Thus the variable material input constitutes a sizeable number of intermediate products and there is considerable variation with respect to price changes in these.

In order to construct a price index for raw materials Apte (1983) takes a weighted average of prices of a small group of important materials which taken together account for a large chunk ($\geq 75\%$) of expenditure on non-energy materials. The weights used were the shares of the items in the total materials considered. Balakrishnan and Pushpangadan (1994) also take a weighted average of price indices of components. However, the weights used are derived from the coefficients of the Input-Output (I-O) Table 1973-74 [Government of India (d)]. A similar approach is followed in Basant and Fikkert (1994), Goldar (2000), Pradhan and Barik (1998, 1999a, 199b), Rao (1996) and Trivedi, Prakash and Sinate (2000) by using I-O Tables for various years[27].

The use of an I-O table in the above mentioned studies has been criticised on the following grounds: *(i)* the available I-O table is for total of registered and unregistered sectors whereas the ASI data refer to the registered sector only [Dholakia and Dholakia 1994], and *(ii)* the use of fixed weights derived from a single I-O table does not allow for structural changes in input composition [Ahluwalia 1994]. It is a limitation of data that an I-O table is not available separately for the registered sector. However, I-O tables for the Indian economy are available for the years 1968-69, 1973-74, 1978-79, 1983-84, 1989-90, 1991-92 and 1996-97[28].

As the present study also uses an I-O table to construct a price index of material input, we discuss the procedure in some detail. It may be noted that the I-O table for the Indian economy brought out by CSO provides input-output coefficients for 115 sectors. A shorter table of 60 sectors is also available from the same source, which is derived from the detailed 115-sector table. The production process in the paper industry does not draw inputs from all 115 or 60 sectors so that for many industries the coefficients are zero. Thus there exists a case to re-group these 60 sectors into a smaller number of major input groups.

Table 3.3
Weights Used for Construction of Material Input Index

	Commodity Groups	*Weight Assigned*
1.	Food Articles (1-4,12,14)	0.01
2.	Non-Food Articles (5-11,13)	5.79
3.	Minerals (16-19)	2.90
4.	Food Products (20-23)	0.51
5.	Textiles (24-28)	1.75
6.	Wood Products (29)	0.20
7.	Paper products (30)	67.69
8.	Leather Products (31)	0.04
9.	Rubber Products (32-33)	1.08
10.	Chemical Products (36-39)	12.62
11.	Non-Metallic Mineral Products (40-41)	0.24
12.	Basic Metals (42-43)	4.30
13.	Other Miscellaneous Manufacturing (53)	2.85
	Total	100.00

Note: Figures in parentheses indicate industry groups as per Input-Output Table, 1989-90 [Government of India (d)].

The re-grouping of the 60 sectors in the I-O table into a smaller number of sectors is done according to major WPI groups[29]. Balakrishnan and Pushpangadan (1994) have derived 19 major industry groups from the I-O tables 1973-74 and 1983-84. Keeping in view the fact that some of the input groups have negligible contribution to the production of paper and paper products we take 13 major input groups. For an input group the relevant I-O coefficients are added together so that we get coefficients for all 13 groups. These coefficients are used as weights against the respective WPI of the input groups.

Over the years the structural coefficients for different I-O tables have undergone changes. Of the available tables, the present study takes the I-O table for the year 1989-90 for construction of the material input index as it is close to the average of all I-O tables. By assigning the relevant weights as discussed above we construct the required price index.

Output

The output variable adopted in the study is the gross value of output as given in the ASI. It is defined to include the ex-factory value (i.e., exclusive of taxes and inclusive of subsidies) of products and byproducts manufactured during the accounting year. The output values given in the ASI are at historical prices, which needs to be neutralised for price changes. In the present study we use the WPI of paper and paper products (average of fiscal year to the base 1981-82 = 100) for obtaining gross output at constant prices.

The choice of an appropriate output measure in Indian manufacturing industries has been put to much debate[30] in recent years. The contending variables suitable for output measure are *(i)* value added with single deflation, *(ii)* value added with double deflation, and *(iii)* gross output. While early productivity literature used value added as a measure of output [see, for example, Solow 1957, and Jorgenson and Griliches 1967 among others] recent studies have put equal emphasis on intermediate inputs such as energy and raw material [Jorgenson, Gollop and Fraumeni 1987, for example]. Secondly, according to a study by Pradhan and Barik (1998) a value added function does not exist in the Indian paper industry. Thirdly, the concept of cost used in the study relates to gross output, not gross value added. Thus our output measure is gross value of output as given in ASI, adjusted for price changes by the WPI of paper and paper products.

Costs

The study requires data on total variable cost as well as cost shares of variable inputs. While defining inputs in the previous section we have specified input shares as the ratios of expenditures on specific inputs to total variable cost. The remaining variable, that is variable cost, is defined as the sum of expenditure on labour, energy and material. Thus it includes total emoluments, fuels consumed and materials consumed. It is useful to note that variable cost is taken at historical prices.

Limitations of Data

The present study suffers from certain limitations with respect to sources of data and construction of variables. Some of these limitations pertain to measurement issues and pervade all variables while others are variable specific.

The study covers a period of 25 years starting with 1973-74. It is quite difficult to maintain the same quality of data throughout the period. With developments in information technology, better training of investigators and learning by doing, it is possible that quality of data has improved over time. However, in the absence of any control variable, we ignore issues pertaining to quality of data and assume that inadequate or defective statistical reporting, if at all present, are uniform throughout. Secondly, it is assumed that all the inputs and output used in the production process do not undergo qualitative changes and maintain the same quality throughout. It is very likely that there are qualitative improvements in inputs, particularly capital and labour, over time. In the process, some of the output growth ascribed to productivity growth may be because of qualitative improvements in inputs. Thirdly, infrastructural facilities such as highways and communication facilities play an important role in improving productivity [Mitra, Varoudakis and Veganzones 1998]. However, these intangible inputs are not charged into the input bill of the industry. Thus improvements in these facilities may be influencing rate of productivity growth.

The ASI data, which are used in the study, suffer from non-reporting bias. Although it is statutory on the part of all industrial units to provide production operation data annually many firms do not provide it on various grounds. Although non-reporting results in a simultaneous decline in levels of output and inputs, it may affect productivity estimates to some extent.

Coming to specific variables let us begin with capital input. It is a major limitation of the present study that it assumes capital to be homogeneous while it has distinct identifiable components. Aggregating these components at historical prices, deflating by a single index number and assuming all components to follow a uniform rate of depreciation and longevity may induce some amount of bias into the level of capital input. Moreover, the linear depreciation rate of 4 per cent per annum is arbitrary in the sense that it is based upon value judgements.

The labour variable used in the study, total persons engaged, is a concept of stock whereas its flow counterpart is man-hours used in the production process. However, the ASI does not provide data on man-hours.

The deflator used for estimation of material input at constant prices also has certain limitations. The input-output table, which is used for the construction of materials input deflator is for both the registered and unregistered sector. On the other hand, the study covers the registered sector only, thereby resulting in some bias in the level of material inputs. Secondly, the limitation that structural change is not allowed when a single I-O table is used is applicable to the present study as well.

The output variable used in the study is at ex-factory prices, that is, exclusive of taxes. On the other hand, the WPI used as deflator of output is inclusive of taxes and subsidies. Thus, changes in tax rates may be influencing the rate of productivity growth.

The WPI data used as deflator may be suffering from non-reporting bias, apart from the error due to changes in weight when the base year is shifted. In the case of non-reporting either it is replaced with other units or old data available for previous time period are repeated. Such problems get accentuated when data are taken at a disaggregated level [Subbarao 1999].

Notes

1. Jorgenson, Gollop and Fraumeni (1987) also estimate the revenue share equations derived from a translog production function together with an equation for rate of technological change. Again, in their case the maintained hypothesis is CRTS.
2. According to Kulatilaka (1987) the major sources of error could be *(i)* measurement (of quantity, price and expenditure) error, *(ii)* optimisation error in the sense that producers may not maximise profit or minimise cost, and *(iii)* functional form approximation error such that technology may not follow a translog functional form.
3. Barten (1969) has shown that if estimation is done through the maximum likelihood method the estimates are invariant to the share equation dropped. Kmenta and Gilbert (1968) have

shown that estimates obtained by the iterative form of Zellner's method are equivalent to maximum likelihood estimates.

4. Berndt and Wood (1975) say that since the level of aggregation in their study is total of U. S. the regressors may not be exogenous and regressors may not be uncorrelated with disturbances. In the same spirit Kulatilaka (1987) is of the opinion that for data pertaining to the whole economy K, Y and P_i are likely to be endogenous. However, according to him, for data covering less than the whole economy it is conceivable that some or all of the above variables are exogenous.
5. In the presence of autocorrelation the parameter estimates are unbiased but not efficient. Thus the effect of autocorrelation needs to be purged from the data. However, the limitation of adding an autocorrelation term to the system is that the estimates are not equivalent to that of maximum likelihood method.
6. The term autoregressive is appropriate because (3.6) can be interpreted as the regression of u_t on itself, lagged one period.
7. Strong stationarity implies that u_t has the same distribution for all t so that moments of all orders are the same. However, this is too strong an assumption in empirical work. Rather we assume that the time series is weakly stationary so that its first and second order moments, i.e., mean, variance and all autocovariances are unaffected by a change of time origin. The autocovariances depend only on the lag or time difference between error terms. The data generating process is explosive if $|\rho|>1$.
8. That may appear to be a restrictive assumption as autocorrelation could be different across equations. However, the assumption of a different ρ value for each equation did not alter the results much and made the estimation process quite slow.
9. One of the share equations is dropped in order to avoid the problem of singularity of error covariance matrix. However, the third share equation can be derived using (3.11). We adhere to the result that the estimates are invariant to share equation dropped [Christensen and Greene 1976].
10. The survey is conducted annually under the statutory provisions of the Collection of Statistics Act, 1953 and rules framed thereunder in 1959.
11. A further classification of industries was undertaken in NIC 1987. However, there was a change in the classification scheme between NIC 1970 and NIC 1987 with respect to the paper industry.
12. For data problems in Indian industrial statistics see Pradhan and Saluja (1998) and Nagaraj (1999).
13. This is a summary statistic denoting the level of concentration of market share in the hands of a few companies. The index

takes values between 0 (no concentration) and 1 (monopoly) and is given by $H = s_1^2 + s_2^2 + s_3^2 + ... + s_n^2$ where *H* is the Herfindahl Index and s_i is the market share of the ith firm.

14. These industry groups are defined as follows: 280: Manufacture of pulp, paper and paperboard including manufacture of newsprint; 281: Manufacture of containers and boxes of paper and paperboard; 282: Manufacture of paper and paperboard articles and pulp products not elsewhere covered; and 283: Manufacture of special purpose paper whether or not printed not elsewhere covered.
15. In fact, the provision of broad-banding facilities available to the industry increases such a possibility.
16. There are three main approaches to measurement of capital input, viz., *(i)* cost of input, *(ii)* productive capacity, and *(iii)* contribution to output. The present study confines itself to the cost of input approach. For theoretical discussion on measurement problems see Banerjee (1975) and Goldar (1986).
17. Technological change could be either due to process innovation or product innovation. In the former the same product is being produced through a different process whereas in the latter case a new product is introduced. Technically we should confine ourselves to process innovation only as our objective is to measure technological change in the production process. However, the fact that a particular plant can produce an array of products and that the product-mix may undergo change, provide us some leeway for product innovation also. Thus, in a way, we cover whatever the paper industry produces.
18. In empirical measurement of capital input there are four approaches, viz., *(i)* replacement cost approach, *(ii)* sample survey of engineering data, *(iii)* book value of capital, and iv) estimates derived from capital expenditure series (perpetual inventory method) [Banerjee 1975]. The first two approaches, which are based on the productive capacity method, require first hand data and thus suffer from sampling error. Of the last two approaches, which are based on the cost of input method, the perpetual inventory method is used in most of the studies [Ahluwalia 1985 &1991; Banerjee 1975; Goldar 1986; Balakrishnan and Pushpangadan 1984; Basant and Fikkert 1996; Pradhan and Barik 1998]. However, some studies have taken book value of fixed capital as a measure of capital stock [for example, Majumdar 1996].
19. Hashim and Dadi (1973) do not provide GNR for land. They provide GNR for the first three components in Table 3.1 only. The GNR for land is taken from Balakrishnan and Pushpangadan (1994).

20. Hashim and Dadi (1973) present two series of capital stock based on fixed capital and productive capital (= fixed capital + working capital). In the productive capital series they exclude value of land while in fixed capital they exclude land and cash.
21. Exceptions in this regard are Hulten and Srinivasan (1999) and Rao (1996) who take productive capital which includes both fixed capital and working capital. The justifications for this, according to Rao (1996) are that *(i)* working capital plays an important role, and *(ii)* the ratio of working capital to productive capital has not remained constant over time. Working capital as per ASI includes physical working capital and cash deposits in hand and at banks. Physical working capital includes inventories such as materials, fuels and lubricants and stores. It also includes the stock of materials, fuels, etc. purchased expressly for resale as well as goods ready for sale at the end of the accounting year. While not understating the importance of working capital, it is worth mentioning that working capital figures, as reported in ASI, do not represent average holdings of inventories and stock but relate rather to the last working day of the accounting year [Government of India (a)]. Secondly, inventories and stock obviously do not conform with the definition of capital with characteristics described at the beginning of this section.
22. Some of the studies suggest that rate of depreciation is higher when capital is put to more intensive use [see, for example, Bischoff and Kokkelenberg 1987]. Thus in a period of boom when capital stock cannot be expanded in the short-run existing stock is put to more than optimal use. This may result in a higher rate of depreciation. In a period of recession the converse may be true.
23. Assumption of a constant rate of capital discarding over the sample period has the same effect as an equivalent constant rate of depreciation.
24. Also called 'one-hoss-shay' pattern of capital retirement.
25. In a recent paper Goldar (2000) provides for capital discarding at a rate of 2.6 per cent per annum.
26. In Summary Results published for the years 1973-74 to 1979-80 'total persons engaged' was termed 'employees' [Government of India (a)].
27. Balakrishnan and Pushpangadan (1994) point out that changing weights on the basis of Input-Output Table 1983-84 does not change the discounted material input figures substantially so as to alter their conclusions.
28. The I-O table for 1968-69 has a different classification from the rest and falls outside the period covered in the study. I-

O tables for 1991-92 and 1996-97 (projected) are given in the Technical Report to the Eighth Five Year Plan [Government of India 1995].

29. The WPI are taken from 'Index Number of Wholesale Prices' [Government of India (b)]. This source provides data on price indices of industry groups for monthly as well as yearly averages. Data from this source has been compiled in Chandhok (1990) for the period 1973-74 to 1987-88 which is used in the present study. For the remaining period, that is 1988-89 to 1997-98, it relies on the publication 'Index Number of Wholesale Prices'. The study uses the average price index for the financial year (April 1 to March 31) instead of calendar year keeping in view the fact that ASI data cover financial years.
WPI are available with three different base years during the study period, viz., 1970-71, 1981-82 and 1993-94. In order to obtain a synchronised series with a particular base year, price indices in different series have been converted into a single series with base year 1981-82 = 100.

30. See Ahluwalia (1994), Balakrishnan and Pushpangadan (1994, 1995, 1996, 1998), Dholakia and Dholakia (1994, 1995), Pradhan and Barik (1998), Rao (1996) and Sastry (1995). See Chapter 5 for further discussion on this issue.

4

Cost Function Results

In this chapter we analyse the production structure of the Indian paper industry. Particularly, we examine features such as capacity utilisation, economies of scale, mark-up over marginal cost, substitution elasticities and price elasticities. These characteristics are computed from the parameter estimates of a translog variable cost function in the framework discussed in Chapter 2. Thus we begin with the estimates of a translog short-run variable cost function before deriving its production characteristics. It is useful to note that we use annual industry data taken from the ASI for the period 1973-74 to 1997-98.

Estimates of a Translog Variable Cost Function

As per the methodology discussed in Chapter 2 we estimated a translog short-run variable cost function with four inputs, viz., *K*, *L*, *E* and *M*. Out of these, *K* is assumed to be quasi-fixed while others are variable. It can be observed from the specification of the variable cost function given in equation (3.1) in Chapter 3 that there are 28 parameters in the cost function. However, in order to fulfil the linear homogeneity conditions on input prices the cost function is normalised by the price of raw material, P_M. As a result the number of parameters was reduced from 28 to 21 (see equation (3.8)). The remaining parameters are estimated by using the conditions given at (3.2). As mentioned in Chapter 3 the input share equations are added to the system of equations so as to gain greater efficiency. In order to avoid the problem of singularity of the error covariance matrix we drop one of the share equations, that is, the share of raw materials. In addition to the cost function and the share equations we add the inverse output demand equation (2.36), and the market equilibrium condition (3.5). As a result there are 5 equations with 25 parameters which are jointly estimated. The system of equations is estimated by the non-linear maximum likelihood method.

Parameter Estimates

Preliminary estimation of the system of equations discussed above exhibited presence of severe autocorrelation in the equations. The Durbin-Watson statistic of the estimated equations turned out to be close to zero in all the equations indicating positive autocorrelation between successive error terms. In order to purge the effect of autocorrelation we re-estimated the system of equations by assuming presence of first order autocorrelation. In order to make estimation procedure simpler we maintained that the value of the autocorrelation coefficient is same across equations.

Estimates of the parameters in the system of equations are reported in Table 4.1. Of the 25 parameters estimated in the model 12 are statistically significant at the 5 per cent level. All first order coefficients of the estimated cost function, except β_K and β_L, are statistically significant at the 5 per cent level.

The estimated cost function has a good fit as can be inferred from the R-squared statistic presented in Table 4.2 for the equations used in the model. As can be seen from the table the R-squared between actual and estimated levels of lnVC is given at 0.99. In addition to the cost function, the factor share equations also have good fit as the value of R-squared between estimated and actual shares are found to be more than 0.90 in all cases. It is encouraging that both the factor share equations have a high value of R-squared as a low R-squared for share equations is reported in some studies [see for example, Denny and Fuss 1977; Kim and Sachis 1986; Ramaswamy *et al.* 1996]. However, the R-squared between the actual and estimated output share equations is comparatively low at 0.62. The inverse output demand equation, again, has a good fit in the sense that R-squared is found to be 0.99.

Table 4.1
Parameter Estimates of a Translog Variable Cost Function

Parameter	*Estimate*	*t-ratio*
β_0	-1554.8	-2.72*
β_L	0.2839	4.93*
β_E	-0.1671	-1.51
β_Y	-0.8974	-2.84*
β_K	-1.0033	-0.74
β_{YY}	0.4171	3.74*
β_{KK}	0.2619	0.78
β_{LL}	0.0501	3.07*
β_{EE}	0.0566	2.40*
β_{LE}	0.0089	0.67
β_{KL}	-0.0064	-0.84
β_{KE}	0.0457	2.55*
β_{KY}	-0.0398	-0.67
β_t	0.9340	2.79*
β_{tt}	-0.0260	-2.55*
β_{Kt}	-0.0104	-0.41
β_{Lt}	-0.0005	-1.57
β_{Et}	0.0016	0.72
β_{Yt}	-0.0215	-2.96*
β_{LY}	-0.0454	-5.43*
β_{EY}	-0.0302	-1.68
α_0	63.582	3.56*
α_Y	-0.1942	-1.55
α_R	-0.1244	-0.27
α_t	-0.2822	-1.39
ρ	0.9957	291.5*

Notes: The estimates pertain to equation (3.8) in Chapter 3.
*indicates statistical significance at the 5 per cent level.

The remaining autocorrelation problem after purging its effect at the estimation stage is not statistically significant. From Table 4.1 we see that the first-order autocorrelation coefficient between successive error terms in the equations is estimated to be 0.9957, which is statistically significant at the 1 per cent level. The D-W statistics in the estimated equations range between 1.77 for the labour share equation to 2.41 for the estimated cost function equation as can be seen from Table 4.2. It is useful to note that the D-W statistic does not have the standard probability distribution when estimation is by an iterative method and residuals are calculated after adjustment for autocorrelation. Thus reliability of the D-W statistic may be reduced in the present study. However, it serves as a reasonable indicator and we expect its value to be around 2 for cases where autocorrelation is absent. Since the D-W statistics for the estimated equations in the case of the Indian paper industry are close to 2 the possibility of severe autocorrelation is unlikely.

Table 4.2
R-Squared and D-W Statistics

Equation	*R-Squared*	*D-W statistic*
lnVC	0.996	2.41
L-Share	0.986	1.77
E-Share	0.904	2.07
Y-Share	0.624	2.40
Inverse Output Demand	0.988	1.78

Note: Pertains to the translog variable cost function and share equations discussed in the text.

Fulfilment of Consistency Properties

The estimated cost function fulfils most of the requisite consistency properties discussed in Chapter 2. It may be recalled that a well-behaved cost function should be: *(i)* non-decreasing in variable factor prices, *(ii)* non-decreasing in output, *(iii)* non-increasing in quasi-fixed factors, *(iv)* homogeneous of degree one in variable input prices, *(v)* concave in variable input prices, and *(vi)* convex in quasi-fixed factors. In the discussion that follows we report the nature of the estimated cost function in the context of above properties.

The estimated variable cost function was found to be increasing in prices and output. The estimated values of the translog variable cost function are positive at all observations. Moreover, both the estimated factor share equations, viz., labour share and energy share, are found to be positive at all the data points. This implies that that the estimated cost function is monotonically increasing in prices which fulfils the monotonicity condition required for the well-behavedness of the cost function. The first order coefficients for labour price β_L and output β_Y are positive while that for energy, β_E, is negative as can be seen from Table 4.1. Prima facie it appears that variable cost is decreasing in energy price. But, by combining the relevant parameter estimates, the estimated share of energy was found to be positive[1]. Secondly, the estimated cost function is increasing in output as the estimated output share is positive at all observations.

A requirement of the estimated variable cost function is that it should be decreasing in *K* which is tantamount to $\frac{\partial G}{\partial K} < 0$. On estimation, $\frac{\partial G}{\partial K}$ is found to be negative for the period 1973-74 to 1993-94 while for the remaining period, that is, for 1994-95 to 1997-98 it turned out to be positive. Thus the regularity condition $\frac{\partial G}{\partial K} < 0$ was met for 84 per cent of the observations in the study while for the remaining 16 per cent it could not be fulfilled.

An implication of the regularity condition $\frac{\partial G}{\partial K} < 0$ is that an increase in capital stock should reduce total variable cost. However, in empirical studies it has been reported that $\frac{\partial G}{\partial K} < 0$ is not met globally and violation of this condition may take place at certain observations [see for example, Bharadwaj 1994; Park and Kwon 1995]. It has been argued that $\frac{\partial G}{\partial K} > 0$ is consistent with short-run equilibrium if current operating conditions are substantially different from the prevailing or expected conditions at the time of making investment decisions. It is useful to recall from Chapter 1 that the policy environment under which the Indian paper industry operated has undergone radical changes over the study period. The initial expectations under which investment took place during the seventies and eighties were totally different from the prevailing conditions during the nineties. This could partly explain non-fulfilment of the condition $\frac{\partial G}{\partial K} < 0$ during later years.

The convexity of the estimated cost function with respect to the quasi-fixed capital input is indicated by the positivity of $\partial^2 VC/\partial K^2$, which equals to β_{KK}. It can be seen from Table 4.1 that the value of β_{KK} is estimated to be 0.2619. Thus the estimated cost function is convex in capital input.

In order to test for the concavity of the estimated cost function with respect to variable input prices we evaluate its Hessian matrix for negative semi-definiteness. Following Diewert and Wales (1987) we obtained the Hessian matrix as

$$H = A - S + \hat{S}\hat{S}' \qquad ...(4.1)$$

where *H* is the Hessian matrix, *A* is the $n \times n$ parameter matrix with β_{ij} coefficients in the main diagonal, *S* is the $n \times n$ matrix with factor shares in the diagonal, and $\hat{S}$ is the factor share vector.

Evaluation of the matrix given at (4.1) showed that the estimated translog short-run cost function fulfils the concavity conditions at all observations.

From the discussion above we observe that the estimated translog cost function fulfils all required consistency properties except for fulfilment of decreasing nature in capital prices at 16 per cent observations. Hence the estimated translog cost is considered to be well behaved.

Results on Hicks-neutrality, Homotheticity and Homogeneity

On the basis of likelihood ratio tests we reject the hypotheses of homotheticity and homogeneity in the production structure of the Indian paper industry. However, the hypothesis of Hicks-neutrality could not be rejected.

The results of likelihood ratio tests are presented in Table 4.3. It is seen from the table that imposition of restrictions with respect to homotheticity resulted in a chi-squared value of 29.66, which is statistically significant at the 5 per cent level. Similarly, the restriction of homogeneity returned a chi-squared value of 250.04, which again is statistically significant at the 5 per cent. On the other hand, the restriction of Hicks-neutrality showed a chi-squared value of 0.82, which is not statistically significant at the 5 per cent level. This implies that the hypotheses of homotheticity and homogeneity are rejected while that of Hicks-neutrality is not rejected in the case of the Indian paper industry for the study period.

Table 4.3
Results of Likelihood Ratio Tests

Hypothesis	*Likelihood Ratio*	*Degree of Freedom*
Hicks-neutrality	0.82	3
Homotheticity	29.66	3
Homogeneity	250.04	4

Note: The likelihood ratio statistic, which follows a chi-squared distribution (asymptotically), is calculated according to (2.10) in Chapter 2.

Our inference on the feature of Hicks-neutrality in the Indian paper industry is reinforced by the statistical significance of the relevant coefficients of the estimated cost function. From Table 4.1 we see that none of the coefficients which indicate interaction of inputs with the time variable (β_{it}) are statistically significant. This implies that relative factor shares have not undergone significant changes over time. In fact, the raw material input share varied from 66.0 per cent (in 1983-84) to 71.9 per cent (in 1995-96) with an average of 68.9 per cent over the period under consideration. On the other hand, the labour share decreased from 17.1 per cent in 1973-74 to 9.3 per cent in 1997-98 while the energy share increased from 12.2 per cent to 20.8 per cent over the same period. However, such changes in factor shares are not statistically significant as indicated by the likelihood ratio test results.

The results of the likelihood ratio test on homotheticity is again justified by the relevant coefficients of the estimated cost function. It is seen from Table 4.1 that one of the interactive terms between output and input variables (β_{IY}) is statistically significant at the 1 per cent level. This implies that isoquants in the case of the Indian paper industry are not radial projections of one another and an input bias in returns to scale is involved. The statistical significance of β_{LY} supports the conclusion that the production function in the industry is not homothetic. In addition, the coefficient β_{YY} is found to be statically significant at the 1 per cent level (see Table 4.1). When seen together with the results of the likelihood ratio test on homotheticity, the statistical significance of β_{YY} supports the view that production function in the case of Indian paper industry is not homogeneous.

Estimates of Capacity Utilisation

Estimates of economic CU obtained from the cost side (CU_C) for the Indian paper industry are presented in Table 4.4. Analysis of the CU given in the table on a yearly basis provides us with three major observations. First, there is under-utilisation of capacity in the Indian paper industry over the period 1973-74 to 1997-98. It is seen from the table that the Indian paper industry has not been in a position to utilise its capacity fully throughout the period of study. In fact, the rate of CU never exceeded unity, a theoretical possibility (see Chapter 2 for details). The highest rate of CU that the industry could reach is found to be 81.86 per cent in 1973-74 while the average over the period of study is 75.45 per cent.

Second, capacity utilisation in the industry has not remained at the same level over the period of study. It is seen from Table 4.4 that CU_C has varied between 81.86 per cent in 1973-74 to 70.53 per cent in 1994-95. The variation in the rate of CU is seen more closely when the rate is plotted against time (see Fig. 4.1). We observe a decline in the rate of CU over the period of study, although fluctuation in CU is a prominent feature of the industry.

Third, the industry experienced a general decline over time in the rate of CU. It is seen from Table 4.4 that CU_C decreased from 81.86 per cent in 1973-74 to 76.94 per cent in 1997-98. However, such a decrease has not been at a uniform rate and fluctuations over the period of study is observed (see Fig. 4.1).

In Table 4.4 we present the traditional capacity utilisation rate (CU_T) along with CU_C. It is observed from the table that CU_T, like CU_C, exhibits a declining trend. Secondly, CU_C returns a higher value than CU_T except for 1974-75 and 1976-

79. Earlier studies also have reported higher values for CU_C than CU_T [see for example, Berndt and Morrison 1981; Morrison 1988, Nelson 1989]. Thirdly, there is a close relationship between both the CU measures as the correlation coefficient between CU_T and CU_C for the period 1973-74 to 1996-97 was found to be 0.71.

Table 4.4

Rate of Capacity Utilisation in Paper Industry: 1973-98

(in per cent)

Year	CU_C	CU_T
1973-74	81.86	81.10
1974-75	79.30	82.29
1975-76	78.23	77.08
1976-77	78.08	84.07
1977-78	78.84	82.23
1978-79	77.22	78.76
1979-80	78.91	75.26
1980-81	74.14	71.94
1981-82	75.03	74.68
1982-83	73.36	63.86
1983-84	72.84	63.26
1984-85	72.79	65.51
1985-86	77.02	64.35
1986-87	75.34	62.93
1987-88	74.91	65.01
1988-89	73.78	63.38
1989-90	78.38	64.27
1990-91	76.68	66.57
1991-92	71.19	65.40
1992-93	71.41	64.66
1993-94	72.53	60.74
1994-95	70.53	66.14
1995-96	73.63	67.74
1996-97	73.38	71.63
1997-98	76.94	—

Notes: CU_C pertains to the dual cost capacity utilisation measure estimated in the study while CU_T is the traditional measure. CU_T values for the years 1973-87 are taken from Chandhok (1990) and for the years 1988-97 are from RBI (a). CU_T for the year 1997-98 is not available from this source.

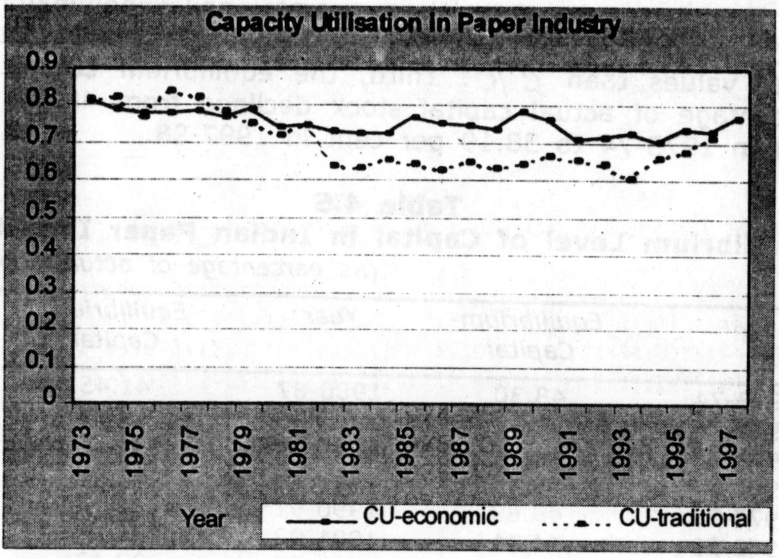

Fig. 4.1

The inference on under-utilisation of capacity gets reinforced when we compare the level of equilibrium capital stock with the actual level. It may be recalled that we obtained the equilibrium level of capital stock by applying Hotelling's lemma to the long-run total cost function and solving it numerically (see Chapter 2). We present the ratio of equilibrium capital stock to its observed value in Table 4.5 and make three observations on the basis of the table. First, the estimated levels of the equilibrium capital have been less than the actual capital throughout the period of study. The equilibrium capital as a percentage of actual capital ranged from 50.72 per cent in 1974-75 to 33.13 per cent in 1992-93. Thus there is an under-utilisation of capital input, which supports our earlier observation of under-utilisation of capacity. Second, there is a discrepancy between the range of capacity utilisation and the utilisation of capital input. The CU ranged from 81.86 per cent in 1973-74 to 70.53 per cent in 1994-95 (see Table 4.4), which is higher than the range of equilibrium capital as a percentage of the actual capital. The discrepancy could be because of the fact that CU_C $(=C^*/C)$ is obtained by adding the variable costs to both the numerator and denominator in $P_K K^* / P_K K$ (see (2.15) in Chapter 2). Thus K^* / K will assume lower values than C^* / C. Third, the equilibrium capital as percentage of actual capital stock declined from 48.30 per cent in 1973-74 to 38.19 per cent in 1997-98.

Table 4.5

Equilibrium Level of Capital in Indian Paper Industry

(as percentage of actual capital)

Year	*Equilibrium Capital*	*Year*	*Equilibrium Capital*
1973-74	48.30	1986-87	41.45
1974-75	50.72	1987-88	40.31
1975-76	48.78	1988-89	39.74
1976-77	49.46	1989-90	41.47
1977-78	49.89	1990-91	40.30
1978-79	44.41	1991-92	34.54
1979-80	47.95	1992-93	33.13
1980-81	42.75	1993-94	34.13
1981-82	43.36	1994-95	34.79
1982-83	39.60	1995-96	34.43
1983-84	40.95	1996-97	35.23
1984-85	40.99	1997-98	38.19
1985-86	41.92	—	—

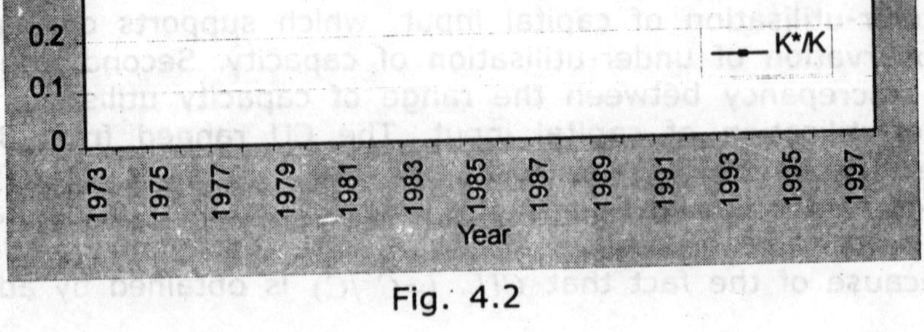

Fig. 4.2

The ratio of equilibrium capital to actual capital is plotted against time in Fig. 4.2. It is observed from the figure that the ratio of equilibrium to actual capital has been less than unity throughout the period implying under-utilisation of existing capital input.

The under-utilisation of capacity observed in the case of the Indian paper industry has several implications. First, excess capacity in the industry implies that scarce resources such as capital are not being utilised fully. Second, the traditional TFP measure that we obtain through Divisia-Tornquist approximation is an under-estimate of true technological change. Had there been full utilisation of capacity, the output growth rate could have been higher. Given the input growth rate, this would reflect a higher growth rate of TFP. Third, the shadow price of capital, which the industry perceives to be the real cost of existing capital, is lower than the prevailing market price at which the industry procures capital. Fourth, as CU is measured along the short-run average cost curve, $CU_C < 1$ indicates that production in the paper industry takes place to the left of the minimum point of the SRAC curve and induces the industry to reduce its capital stock in the long-run.

The growth rate in capital stock over the period of study has been 7.49 per cent per annum. Logically under-utilisation of capacity should induce the industry to reduce capital stock. However, the industry has experienced negative net investment during 4 years, viz., 1985-86, 1989-90, 1995-96 and 1997-98. In these years the book value of fixed capital has declined over that of the previous year[2]. This assumes importance in view of the fact that there have been reports on closure of unviable units [RBI (a)]. Thus the industry could have found a route to disinvestment through closure of such units.

Estimates of Scale Economies

The Indian paper industry is found to have exploited the benefits of scale economies during the period of study. In the short-run, the degree of returns to scale varied within the range 1.87 in the year 1974-75 to 1.55 in 1981-82 and 1995-96 (see Table 4.6).

We present estimates of long-run returns to scale in Table 4.5 on the basis of the relationship between SRTS and CU as discussed in Chapter 2. It is seen from the table that the Indian paper industry experienced economies of scale throughout the period of study. The degree of LRTS registered by the industry has varied from 1.55 in 1974-75 to 1.14 in 1995-96 (see Table 4.6). Secondly, along with fluctuations, a general decline is observed in the degree of returns to scale (see Fig. 4.3).

Table 4.6
Degree of Returns to Scale in Paper Industry: 1973-98

Year	*SRTS*	*LRTS*
1973-74	1.68	1.45
1974-75	1.87	1.55
1975-76	1.68	1.36
1976-77	1.69	1.37
1977-78	1.65	1.35
1978-79	1.73	1.38
1979-80	1.67	1.36
1980-81	1.68	1.26
1981-82	1.55	1.18
1982-83	1.83	1.36
1983-84	1.81	1.33
1984-85	1.66	1.21
1985-86	1.80	1.40
1986-87	1.77	1.34
1987-88	1.86	1.40
1988-89	1.81	1.34
1989-90	1.63	1.29
1990-91	1.58	1.22
1991-92	1.71	1.22
1992-93	1.86	1.33
1993-94	1.86	1.35
1994-95	1.69	1.18
1995-96	1.55	1.14
1996-97	1.62	1.19
1997-98	1.72	1.32

The presence of scale economies in the industry needs to be interpreted in terms of the average cost (AC) curve facing it. As returns to scale is equivalent to the ratio of average cost to marginal cost[3] (MC), the presence of scale economies indicates divergence between the two and $AC > MC$. This is possible when production takes place in the downward sloping segment of AC curve. Secondly, decline in the degree of scale economies implies that the gap between AC and MC is getting narrowed down over time.

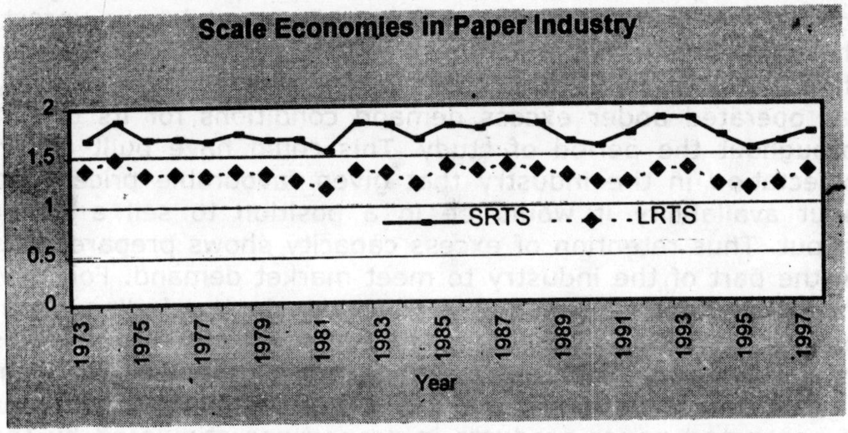

Fig. 4.3

Scale economies estimated in the present study pertains to aggregate industry level data. Thus they need to be interpreted with caution. Usually scale economies represent the responsiveness of production cost to increase in size of firm estimated from cross-section data. In time series data presence of scale economies implies that as the size of the industry increases it becomes more cost-effective, as average cost declines. The presence of scale economies in the case of the Indian paper industry could be an outcome of better infrastructure such as roads, transport and communication, and improvement in market density arising out of growth in population, purchasing power and literacy.

The presence of scale economies along with under-utilisation of capacity in the industry is a somewhat baffling result of the present study. It is useful to note that paper and paper products are more or less homogeneous in nature, as the product of one firm is not distinguished from that of others. Moreover, consumers view products of one firm as close substitutes for those of others. In such circumstances maintaining excess capacity is tantamount to reducing competition by posing artificial entry barriers. Thus under-utilisation of capacity could be a reflection of a production strategy in the industry. Secondly, the production process in the Indian paper industry is often interrupted by irregular flow of raw material and energy, and frequent labour unrest. This interrupts production and capacity is not fully utilised. Thirdly, as observed in Chapter 1, the Indian paper industry has operated under excess demand conditions for its output throughout the period of study. This could have built up an expectation in the industry that given favourable prices and input availability it would be in a position to sell a larger output. Thus retention of excess capacity shows preparedness on the part of the industry to meet market demand. Fourthly, the pricing mechanism and product-mix in the Indian paper industry were regulated during the seventies and early eighties by the government through paper control orders issued from time to time. This required firms to produce different varieties of paper and paper products in proportions stipulated by the government. The non-viability of such restrictions from a market demand point of view could have worked as a discouraging factor for utilising capacity fully.

Estimate of Mark-up

We estimated the inverse-output demand function along with the translog variable cost function and share equations. Such a procedure provided us with an estimate of α_Y, which represents the effect of changes in output on price such that $\alpha_Y = \dfrac{\partial \ln P_Y}{\partial \ln Y}$.

In the present study α_Y turned out to be -0.2328 with t-value of -1.55 for the Indian paper industry. By applying the estimate of α_Y to the equation for estimation of mark-up (refer to the equation (2.39) in Chapter 2), i.e.,

$$\theta = \frac{P_Y - MC}{P_Y} = \frac{-\alpha_Y}{1+\alpha_Y}$$

we obtain a value of 0.3034. Thus the estimated mark-up over marginal cost is found to be 30.34 per cent in the Indian paper industry.

The estimated mark-up over marginal cost in the Indian paper industry indicates that the price of paper and paper products has been higher than the marginal cost of production. This could be because of the imperfection present in the industry. However, according to the CMIE (1999) the Herfindahl index in the industry was 0.01 in 1997-98, which indicated an absence of concentration in the industry. In fact, the Indian paper industry comprises a large number of paper mills each contributing a small fraction to the industry output. The largest two firms in the industry, for example, produced 6.47 per cent and 3.13 per cent of total output in 1997-98 [CMIE 1999]. Thus the presence of mark-up in the industry may not be due to monopoly power and we have to look for alternative explanations.

It is a limitation of the data used in the study that the output price is taken from the WPI which includes indirect taxes while the variable cost is exclusive of indirect taxes and subsidies (see Chapter 3). Thus the rate of indirect taxes imposed on the industry may influence the mark-up. The Indian paper industry has been subjected to multiplicity of indirect taxes at different levels of administration. The central government imposes central excise duties while the state governments impose sales taxes on paper and paper product. While the rate of central excise tax has varied over time, the rate of sales tax has varied across years and states. Variations in the rates of these taxes influence the movements in the WPI. Secondly, the government has been able to influence the price of paper and paper products by *(i)* directly fixing the price as a number of paper mills are in the public sector, and *(ii)* imposing restrictions on paper prices through the paper control orders. Thus the observed price of paper and paper products may not be on the basis of cost of production.

Mark-up for the Indian manufacturing industries has been estimated by Srivastava (1996) on the basis of Hall's methodology as applied to firm level data. According to that study the price-marginal cost ratio in the Indian paper industry was in the range of 0.99 to 1.01 during the period 1980-81 to 1989-90. We found the result of the present study to be a relatively higher estimate, which could be ascribed to the following reasons: one, we include the controlled policy period in addition to the liberalised one (1973-98) whereas Srivastava's study pertains to the more or less liberalised regime (1980-90). It is useful to note that partial de-licensing in the Indian paper industry started during the early eighties. Thus the possibility of higher mark-up during the controlled regime could not be ruled out. Two, the method of analysis and coverage of the present study is different from that of Srivastava, which also accounts for the difference. While Srivastava (1996) takes a sample of public limited companies we take the entire factory sector. Moreover, we resort to a translog variable cost function model where factor share, market equilibrium and inverse output demand equations are added at the estimation stage. On the other hand, Srivastava's result is based on a modified Solow residual in line with Hall (1988, 1990).

Estimates of Substitution Elasticities

Estimates of short-run and long-run APES for the Indian paper industry (symbolised by *A*, with appropriate subscripts) are presented in Table 4.7 and Table 4.8 respectively. It is seen from Table 4.7, which gives the short-run APES, that labour, energy and material inputs are substitutes for one another in the short-run. It is observed from the table that these inputs continue to remain substitutes to one another throughout the period of study. Such substitution possibilities offer some scope to the producers for increasing production by using inputs which are easily available. Secondly, there is a gradual decline in the values of the APES between energy and raw material and that between labour and material. On the other hand, the APES values between labour and energy have remained mostly unchanged. Thirdly, the own substitution elasticities of all the variable inputs, viz., *L*, *E* and *M* are negative. This indicates that an increase in the price of an input results in relatively lesser use of the concerned input. Such a feature reflects the well-behavedness of the estimated variable cost function.

Table 4.7
Short-run APES in Indian Paper Industry: 1973-98

Year	A_{LE}	A_{LM}	A_{EM}	A_{LL}	A_{EE}	A_{MM}
1973-74	1.43	8.79	11.86	-3.14	-3.39	-4.16
1974-75	1.41	9.05	11.11	-3.20	-3.33	-4.23
1975-76	1.37	9.29	10.29	-3.23	-3.19	-4.39
1976-77	1.36	9.70	9.69	-3.32	-3.07	-4.45
1977-78	1.36	9.92	9.49	-3.38	-3.03	-4.45
1978-79	1.32	9.86	9.08	-3.30	-2.89	-4.71
1979-80	1.38	10.26	9.43	-3.49	-3.04	-4.34
1980-81	1.37	10.86	8.77	-3.59	-2.86	-4.46
1981-82	1.38	11.52	8.43	-3.72	-2.77	-4.43
1982-83	1.32	11.48	7.92	-3.64	-2.53	-4.85
1983-84	1.32	11.87	7.74	-3.70	-2.47	-4.87
1984-85	1.36	12.79	7.61	-3.86	-2.46	-4.68
1985-86	1.35	12.44	7.74	-3.82	-2.51	-4.66
1986-87	1.40	13.55	7.64	-3.95	-2.52	-4.46
1987-88	1.38	13.97	7.35	-3.96	-2.39	-4.61
1988-89	1.39	14.31	7.33	-3.98	-2.40	-4.56
1989-90	1.48	15.54	7.54	-3.94	-2.56	-4.18
1990-91	1.49	15.90	7.47	-3.91	-2.54	-4.18
1991-92	1.51	15.31	7.79	-3.94	-2.67	-4.05
1992-93	1.47	15.76	7.36	-3.94	-2.47	-4.28
1993-94	1.44	15.73	7.22	-3.95	-2.40	-4.39
1994-95	1.48	16.62	7.22	-3.85	-2.43	-4.27
1995 -96	1.58	16.54	7.85	-3.77	-2.73	-3.89
1996-97	1.49	16.50	7.32	-3.85	-2.48	-4.21
1997-98	1.45	16.11	7.13	-3.93	-2.36	-4.42

Note: A in the table represents APES.

It is worth mentioning that our results on short-run APES are in line with the results obtained in Ramaswamy et al. (1996)[4] although degree of substitutability is found to be relatively higher in the present study. This could be because of the following reasons: *(i)* our study covers pulp and paper while that of Ramaswamy et al. (1996) is only for the waste paper based paper mills, *(ii)* our study takes time series aggregate data from ASI while that of Ramaswamy et al. (1996) is based on cross-section primary data of a small sample of firms.

Analysis of the long-run APES between pairs of inputs indicate that all the variable inputs considered in the study, viz., labour, energy and material, are substitutes for one another. This reinforces our earlier results obtained for the short-run substitution elasticities. In this case also, the extent of substitutability between material and energy, and labour and material was found to be higher compared to that between labour and energy. Own price elasticities for variable inputs were found to be negative indicating the well-behavedness of the estimated cost function.

Table 4.8
Long-run APES in Indian Paper Industry: 1973-98

Year	A_{LL}	A_{EE}	A_{MM}	A_{LE}	A_{LM}	A_{EM}	A_{KL}	A_{KE}	A_{KM}
1973-74	-3.83	-4.15	-5.08	1.75	10.74	14.49	0.17	-1.75	0.26
1974-75	-3.77	-3.92	-4.99	1.66	10.66	13.09	0.17	-1.56	0.25
1975-76	-4.20	-4.16	-5.72	1.79	12.09	13.39	0.19	-1.56	0.28
1976-77	-4.32	-3.99	-5.78	1.77	12.61	12.59	0.20	-1.44	0.29
1977-78	-4.49	-4.03	-5.91	1.81	13.18	12.62	0.21	-1.44	0.29
1978-79	-4.18	-3.65	-5.96	1.68	12.48	11.49	0.19	-1.27	0.29
1979-80	-4.49	-3.91	-5.58	1.78	13.20	12.13	0.21	-1.40	0.28
1980-81	-4.83	-3.84	-5.99	1.83	14.59	11.78	0.23	-1.33	0.29
1981-82	-4.79	-3.57	-5.70	1.77	14.82	10.85	0.24	-1.23	0.28
1982-83	-5.39	-3.75	-7.19	1.96	17.03	11.74	0.26	-1.26	0.34
1983-84	-5.04	-3.36	-6.63	1.80	16.16	10.54	0.25	-1.13	0.31
1984-85	-5.35	-3.41	-6.48	1.88	17.71	10.54	0.28	-1.14	0.31
1985-86	-5.05	-3.32	-6.16	1.79	16.44	10.23	0.26	-1.12	0.30
1986-87	-5.09	-3.25	-5.74	1.80	17.45	9.83	0.29	-1.09	0.28
1987-88	-5.29	-3.19	-6.16	1.84	18.64	9.80	0.30	-1.07	0.30
1988-89	-5.31	-3.20	-6.09	1.86	19.11	9.78	0.31	-1.07	0.30
1989-90	-5.12	-3.32	-5.43	1.92	20.18	9.79	0.34	-1.12	0.28
1990-91	-5.12	-3.32	-5.47	1.95	20.82	9.79	0.36	-1.12	0.28
1991-92	-5.46	-3.70	-5.61	2.08	21.18	10.79	0.37	-1.26	0.29
1992-93	-5.38	-3.38	-5.85	2.00	21.53	10.06	0.36	-1.13	0.29
1993-94	-5.28	-3.20	-5.86	1.93	21.00	9.64	0.35	-1.07	0.29
1994-95	-5.56	-3.50	-6.16	2.14	23.99	10.43	0.41	-1.17	0.31
1995-96	-5.23	-3.79	-5.39	2.19	22.95	10.89	0.41	-1.30	0.29
1996-97	-5.46	-3.51	-5.96	2.12	23.38	10.37	0.40	-1.18	0.30
1997-98	-4.94	-2.97	-5.55	1.82	20.24	8.96	0.34	-0.99	0.27

Note: A in the table represents APES.

Capital is found to be a complement to energy in the case of the Indian paper industry. The degree of complementarity between capital and energy was found to be relatively high (see Table 4.8). However, its degree has decreased over the years.

Keeping in view the fact that the production process in the paper industry is energy intensive (the energy bill accounts for about 20 per cent of total variable cost), *K-E* complementarity[5] holds important policy implications. First, capital and energy are utilised to some extent in a fixed proportion. Thus the possibility of reducing the level of energy consumption and compensating such reduction through increased capital input is quite remote. Second, an increase in the price of energy is expected to retard the rate of investment and capital formation in the industry. Third, a decrease in the price of energy would have the favourable effect of accelerating capital investment, but this in turn would be accompanied by additional energy demand.

Our estimates on short-run and long-run APES satisfy the Le Chatelier principle. According to this principle, the own price response of variable inputs decline as the number of quasi-fixed factors increase. In the present study there is one quasi-fixed input, that is capital, whose level can be adjusted to equilibrium in the long-run. Thus short-run own price elasticities should be lower in absolute terms in the short-run than in the long-run. Comparison of estimates of A_{LL}, A_{EE} and A_{MM} in the short-run (see Table 4.7) and in the long-run (see Table 4.8) shows that short-run estimates are lower than long-run estimates (in absolute terms) for all the years.

Estimates of Price Elasticities

We find that the own price responses of all the variable inputs, viz., labour, energy and material, are negative, as expected of a well-behaved cost function (see Table 4.9). Of the three variable inputs, the price elasticities of labour and energy were found to be less than unity in absolute terms for all the years. This implies inelasticity of these two inputs. On the other hand, the price elasticity of raw material was found to be more than unity in absolute terms for all the years, which implies elasticity. Thus the industry is quite sensitive to price changes in raw material.

The price elasticity of material inputs with respect to energy was found to be quite high. This implies that an increase in energy prices has a strong influence on the use of more raw materials. Similarly, the price elasticity of energy with respect to material was found to be elastic, although its degree was lower.

Table 4.9
Price Elasticities of Demand in Indian Paper Industry: 1973-98

Year	A_{LE}	A_{EL}	A_{LM}	A_{ML}	A_{EM}	A_{ME}	A_{LL}	A_{EE}	A_{MM}
1973-74	0.30	0.21	1.83	7.60	1.76	10.26	-0.65	-0.50	-3.59
1974-75	0.28	0.22	1.78	7.48	1.72	9.18	-0.63	-0.52	-3.50
1975-76	0.29	0.26	1.99	8.34	1.95	9.24	-0.69	-0.61	-3.94
1976-77	0.28	0.28	1.99	8.64	1.98	8.63	-0.68	-0.63	-3.96
1977-78	0.28	0.29	2.03	9.04	2.03	8.65	-0.69	-0.65	-4.05
1978-79	0.27	0.29	1.99	8.33	1.99	7.67	-0.67	-0.63	-3.98
1979-80	0.26	0.28	1.93	9.15	1.94	8.41	-0.66	-0.63	-3.87
1980-81	0.26	0.32	2.03	9.99	2.07	8.07	-0.67	-0.67	-4.10
1981-82	0.23	0.32	1.93	10.17	1.99	7.45	-0.62	-0.65	-3.92
1982-83	0.27	0.40	2.32	11.21	2.41	7.73	-0.74	-0.77	-4.73
1983-84	0.24	0.38	2.13	10.62	2.23	6.92	-0.66	-0.71	-4.36
1984-85	0.22	0.40	2.11	11.86	2.23	7.06	-0.64	-0.72	-4.34
1985-86	0.22	0.37	2.02	11.03	2.11	6.87	-0.62	-0.69	-4.13
1986-87	0.20	0.37	1.91	11.95	2.02	6.74	-0.56	-0.67	-3.93
1987-88	0.20	0.40	2.01	12.56	2.14	6.60	-0.57	-0.70	-4.15
1988-89	0.19	0.41	1.99	12.95	2.13	6.63	-0.55	-0.70	-4.13
1989-90	0.18	0.39	1.85	14.25	1.98	6.91	-0.47	-0.67	-3.83
1990-91	0.17	0.40	1.86	14.71	2.00	6.91	-0.46	-0.68	-3.86
1991-92	0.19	0.40	1.95	15.17	2.07	7.72	-0.50	-0.71	-4.02
1992-93	0.18	0.42	1.97	15.03	2.12	7.02	-0.49	-0.71	-4.08
1993-94	0.18	0.42	1.95	14.48	2.10	6.65	-0.49	-0.70	-4.04
1994-95	0.18	0.46	2.07	16.77	2.24	7.29	-0.48	-0.75	-4.31
1995-96	0.18	0.41	1.90	16.76	2.04	7.95	-0.43	-0.71	-3.94
1996-97	0.18	0.44	2.02	16.45	2.18	7.30	-0.47	-0.74	-4.20
1997-98	0.16	0.40	1.83	13.92	1.99	6.17	-0.45	-0.66	-3.82

In order to have a clearer picture of the effects of individual input price increases we present the results of a 1 per cent increase in all the inputs on the demand for other inputs. As we see from Table 4.10, a 1 per cent increase in the wage rate tends to increase demand for raw material by 2.01 per cent. Similarly a 1 per cent increase in energy price has an impact of increasing material input demand by 2.09 per cent. On the other hand, a 1 per cent increase in the material input price has the positive effect of increasing employment by 11.45 per cent. But such an increase is expected to boost energy consumption by 7.59 per cent.

Table 4.10
Effect of Input Price Rise on other Inputs

1 per cent increase in price of	*percentage change in quantity of* K	L	E	M
L	0.03	-0.63	0.23	2.01
E	-0.24	0.34	-0.69	2.09
M	0.20	11.45	7.59	-4.10

Note: Values in the table relate to mean-level factor shares and costs estimated at equilibrium level of capital stock.

Thus we conclude that the Indian paper industry has not been able to utilise its capital stock optimally. Estimates of the economic capacity utilisation rate indicate gross under-utilisation of capacity in the industry. The average rate of capacity utilisation in the industry during 1973-98 has been 75.45 per cent. Secondly, there is a general decline in the rate of capacity utilisation in the industry over the period of study. For a developing economy such as India such under-utilisation amounts to wastage of scarce resources.

Analysis of short-run elasticities indicates that labour, energy and material inputs are substitutes for one another. Of these, raw material is highly substitutable with energy and labour. Own price elasticities of all the variable inputs are negative, which indicate that an increase in the price of an input results in relatively less use of the input under consideration. Such a feature of own price elasticities reflects the well-behavedness of the estimated variable cost function.

The long-run APES between pairs of inputs indicate that

all the variable inputs considered in the study are substitutes for one another. This reinforces our earlier results obtained for the short-run substitution elasticities.

Capital is found to be a complement to energy in the case of the Indian paper industry. Keeping in view the fact that the production process in the paper industry is energy intensive *K-E* complementarity indicates difficulties in reducing the level of energy consumption through increased capital input. Moreover, an increase in the price of energy is likely to retard the rate of investment in the industry. While a decrease in the price of energy would accelerate capital investment, it would be accompanied by additional energy demand.

Of the three variable inputs, the price elasticity of raw material was found to be more than unity in absolute terms for all the years. On the other hand, the price elasticities of labour and energy were found to be less than unity in absolute terms for the study period. Thus the industry is sensitive to price changes in raw material. From the analysis of cross-elasticities of demand we infer that a 1 per cent increase in the wage rate tends to increase demand for raw material by 2.01 per cent. Similarly a 1 per cent increase in energy price has the effect of increasing material input demand by 2.09 per cent. On the other hand, a 1 per cent increase in the material input price has the positive effect of increasing employment by 11.45 per cent. But such an increase is expected to increase energy consumption by 7.59 per cent.

An implication of the above is that the possibility of a trade off between exhaustible (*E, M*) and non-exhaustible (*K, L*) inputs is remote. If we increase the price of raw material, energy consumption will go up, although it will generate additional employment. On the other hand, if we increase the price of energy there will be an increase in raw material consumption. However, it is useful to note that an increase in the prices of both energy and raw material would generate additional employment.

Notes

1. It is worth mentioning that $\beta_{l:}$ was positive in the initial estimation when we did not allow for autocorrelation between error terms.

But on re-estimation with first order autocorrelation this turns out to be negative.

2. The difference in book values of fixed capital for successive years is taken as a measure of net investment. See Chapter 3 for details.
3. It can be shown that $-\eta^{-1} = \dfrac{1}{\partial \ln C/\partial \ln Y} = \dfrac{C/Y}{\partial C/\partial Y} = \dfrac{AC}{MC}$
4. The study by Ramaswamy et al. (1996) estimates a constant returns to scale variable cost function with an embedded materials sub-model. The purpose of the study is to find substitution elasticities between inputs. A major limitation of the study is that it does not attempt to estimate long-run APES when capital stock is adjusted to its equilibrium level.
5. The issue of *K-E* complementarity has been long debated in the literature. Particularly, attempts have been made to reconcile *(i)* econometric findings of *K-E* complementarity and engineering notions of *K-E* substitutability, and *(ii)* short-run complementarity and long-run substitutability. These issues, however, are beyond the scope of the present study. See, among others, Berndt (1976), Berndt and Wood (1979, 1981), Griffin and Gregory (1976) and Griffin (1981).

Part II
Productivity Growth

5

Approaches to Productivity Measurement

Major developments in the sphere of productivity analysis evolved through the second half of the twentieth century. However, the concept of productivity can be traced back to a study by Copeland and Martin (1938) [Griliches 1996] in which they suggested that comparing value of total inputs to value of total output would provide a 'rough measure of changes in the efficiency of our economic system'. It was Tinbergen (1942) who added a time trend to the usual Cobb-Douglas production function representing the level of 'efficiency' in a notable but neglected article published in German in 1942 [Krishna 1987; Griliches 1996]. In the mean time, the notion of efficiency or total factor productivity (TFP) was introduced independently by Stigler (1947) which generated a lot of interest.

The concept of TFP [Tinbergen 1942, Stigler 1947], which takes into account all the factors of production used in the production process, is used frequently as a measure of productive efficiency. According to Kendrick (1961) productivity estimates can be useful *(i)* as a means of motivating efficiency, *(ii)* as a basis for prediction and policy formulation, and *(iii)* in establishing dynamic economic relationships.

Within the ambit of production analysis, TFP is defined as a shift in the production function [Solow 1957] and should be distinguished from movements along a production function. It is recognised in the early literature that changes in inputs cannot explain fully the changes in output, even if constant returns prevails. Thus the growth rate in output is not always equal to the growth rate in total inputs. The remainder of output growth after allowing for the growth rate in inputs is ascribed to the growth rate in TFP and is often termed 'The Residual' or 'The Measure of Our Ignorance' [Jorgenson and Griliches 1967].

The concept of TFP, postulated as a residual, crucially depends upon fulfilment of certain restrictive assumptions such as constant returns to scale, full utilisation of capacity and presence of perfect competition in the product market. In cases when these conditions are not met, TFP includes the effects of scale economies, capacity utilisation and mark-up over marginal cost. Nonetheless, the effects of these factors can be purged from TFP and for this purpose we require appropriate estimates of various characteristics that describe production structure of the industry.

Economic literature offers three broad approaches to productivity measurement[1] [Christensen 1980; Diewert 1980], viz., *(i)* index number approach, *(ii)* econometric approach, and *(iii)* non-parametric approach[2]. As will be seen in the following discussion, each of these approaches has its respective strengths and weaknesses[3]. The process of estimating productivity requires a basic assumption that technology follows a certain structure which may be at variance with empirical data analysis. Thus productivity estimates by one method need to be reinforced by those from others [Christensen 1980].

Index Number Approach

Productivity measures can be either partial or total. A partial factor productivity (PFP) index [Good, Nadiri and Sickles 1997] can be constructed for each of the inputs used in the production of output. Such a measure describes average product of the input considered. A limitation of the PFP measures is that it is dependent upon the level of other inputs used. For example, application of higher doses of capital increases the labour productivity measure even if the quantity and character of labour input do not change. This limitation of PFP can be overcome by taking into account the levels of all inputs used in production of the output.

Based on what constitutes output and inputs Kendrick

distinguishes between TFP and total productivity (TP) [OECD 1991]. According to him TP is the ratio of gross output to all associated tangible inputs—labour, capital, and intermediate products—while TFP is the ratio of real (final) product to real inputs. Thus TFP excludes intermediate inputs from both the numerator and denominator. However, such a convention has not been followed in the literature and both terms are being used interchangeably [see, for example, Kennedy and Thirlwal, 1972; Park and Kwon 1995; Sato and Ramachandran 1980]. In the sense of Kendrick the present study is one on TP.

The index number approach has the advantage that it does not require direct estimation of an underlying production function. It takes the production function merely as an organising device and not an estimating framework and lacks a stochastic term [Felipe 1997]. Therefore, fairly strong assumptions about the underlying technology need to be maintained in the index number approach so as to obtain meaningful estimation of productivity [Good, Nadiri and Sickles 1997]. As parametric specification is not required, the index number approach can accommodate a larger number of inputs and does not require a long data set. If technological change is assumed to be irregular and in spurts, the index number approach is more appropriate than the econometric approach where technological change is smooth [Berndt and Khaled 1979].

The traditional definition of TFP as a ratio between output and inputs can be expressed in terms of growth rates by logarithmic differentiation. By subtracting appropriately weighted input growth rates from output growth rate we obtain a measure of growth rate in TFP[4]. The issue of index numbers arises here as growth rates in inputs[5] are to be combined. These index numbers are expected to fulfil the properties laid out by Fisher (1927) and Diewert[6] (1976). Such a procedure also allows decomposition of the output growth rate as a sum of input growth rates and growth rate in TFP and hence is termed as growth accounting approach.

Depending upon the weights assigned to different components of inputs there are many productivity indices suggested in the literature. These weighting procedures are based on a specific production function. The 'Kendrick index' is obtained if the weights used for combining inputs are arithmetic and the underlying production function is additive linear[7] (Kendrick 1961). If the weights are geometric and the underlying production function is neo-classical, the 'Solow Index' is obtained[8] (Solow 1957). If the input components are combined through a Divisia index we obtain a 'translog index' of productivity[9]. In the productivity literature the translog index is preferred to Kendrick and Solow indices as it is based on a flexible functional form.

The index number approach to productivity measurement rests on certain premises: viz., *(i)* homogeneous inputs which imply no qualitative changes in them[10], *(ii)* perfect competition in the product market, *(iii)* Hicks-neutral technological progress[11], *(iv)* constant returns to scale, *(v)* constant rate of capacity utilisation, and *(vi)* instantaneous adjustment of inputs to their equilibrium levels. On fulfilment of these assumptions TFP would be equivalent to technological change [Solow 1957; Denny, Fuss and Waverman 1981; Morrison 1992]. Conversely, in the event of non-fulfilment of these assumptions, which is more likely in empirical studies, many factors get grouped together with technological progress. Hence, what is measured empirically as TFP is a combination of *(i)* technological progress; *(ii)* scale economies; *(iii)* learning by doing; *(iv)* market power; and *(v)* X-inefficiencies. Felipe (1997) adds managerial capabilities, organisational competence, research and development, inter-sectoral transfer of resources and diffusion of technology to the above list. To pull the strings together, a TFP estimate obtained as a traditional Solow-residual may help assess its trend but does not offer scope for decomposing the underlying components that are responsible for the outcome.

Research on index number based productivity analysis has progressed on two lines: one, decomposing the components of TFP and two, establishing a relationship of TFP with pure technological change which is defined as a shift in the production function [Denny, Fuss and Waverman 1981]. Following Solow (1957), TFP and technological change are being used interchangeably. However, Jorgenson and Griliches (1967) endeavoured to distinguish between these two concepts and in the process isolated the influence of scale economies and measurement error from TFP. Such an approach has been further improved by Denny, Fuss and Waverman (1981), Ohta

(1974) and Morrison (1988, 1992). Apart from the impact of scale economies there are other factors such as mark-up and capacity utilisation which can be isolated from TFP [Morrison 1992]. Thus purging the impact of the above-mentioned factors from the traditional TFP estimate provides us with a more realistic estimate of technological change.

The index number approach pre-imposes many restrictions on technology which can be relaxed in the econometric approach. However, the index number approach is still useful as it provides a good testing ground for measurement of productivity [Good, Nadiri and Sickles 1997].

Econometric Approach

In the econometric approach the first step is to specify a production or its dual, cost (price[12]) function. Under certain regularity conditions the production function and its dual, the cost function, contain identical economically relevant information. The growth rate of TFP estimated econometrically through the production, cost or price function [Jorgenson 1986] offers better insight compared to the one obtained by using the index number approach. It is worth mentioning that the econometric approach offers scope for estimation of scale economies, capacity utilisation and technological bias, which the index number approach does not.

Within the econometric approach some of the studies [see, for example, Bhavani 1991a; Jorgenson *et al.* 1987] have estimated a production function to derive producer behaviour. However, there is a general preference for the cost function over production and price functions because of the following advantages:

(i) In the case of a production (price) function we have to impose constant returns to scale on the structure of technology as we do not have realistic measures of input prices, particularly that of capital. On the other hand, such a restriction can be relaxed in the case of a cost function[13].

(ii) A major advantage of the cost function is that we obtain input demand functions by simple differentiation of the cost function and application of Shephard's lemma. The

estimation of the share equations along with the cost function provides more efficient estimates as degrees of freedom increase.

(iii) The production function assumes input quantities to be exogenously given while the cost function is based on the exogeneity of the quantity of output and prices of inputs. Within a cost function framework the producers are akin to atomistic competitors in the sense that they take input prices as given. Thus, in a market with some elements of competition it is more realistic to assume that input prices are exogenously determined and input quantities are a consciously controlled decision of the firm. In economy-wide models input prices and output levels may not be purely exogenous. However, in disaggregated models such an assumption is not unrealistic.

(iv) In the Marshallian tradition all inputs entering into the production process may not be variable in the short-run. The quasi-fixity of certain inputs in the sense that their levels can be changed only in the long-run can be brought into the analytical structure with a short-run variable cost function only [Lau 1976].

(v) Since the cost function deals with observable market phenomena such as demands, prices, and costs it has natural advantages for applied production analysis [Chambers 1988].

(vi) Finally, investment and other decisions are taken both at the firm and industry levels keeping output projections in view. The firm first projects the level of output for which demand exists and keeping such demand in view either goes for capacity building or operates existing units. Thus formulation of output as an exogenous variable seems more appropriate than taking input quantities as exogenous. In such circumstances a cost function approach is more realistic.

Choice of a Flexible Functional Form

A production function provides information on relevant characteristics of producer behaviour. For smooth technologies (i.e., those that are twice continuously differentiable) such information includes the value of the function, the gradient of the function and the Hessian matrix. In the case of a production function involving n inputs this would imply *(i)* level of output, *(ii)* n marginal productivities, and *(iii)* n^2 elements of the Hessian matrix[14]. These separate effects add up to $\frac{1}{2}(n+1)(n+2)$ in number. In empirical analysis it is seen that the number of parameters depends upon the number of separate effects to be measured. Hence, it requires $\frac{1}{2}(n+1)(n+2)$ number of parameters to be present in a production function so as to measure all these separate effects [Chambers 1988]. The traditional production functions such as Cobb-Douglas and CES put some restrictions on technology[15] as they do not have that many parameters.

The introduction of flexible functional forms has reduced *a priori* restrictions on technology to the minimum. A flexible functional form is a second order approximation[16] to any arbitrary function. In this framework flexibility is defined as the ability of a functional form to represent producer behaviour without imposing any *a priori* restrictions on elasticities. Thus, for a flexible cost function, '...at any given level of non-negative (positive) prices of inputs the parameters of the cost function can be chosen so that the derived ...input demand functions and their own and cross price elasticities are capable of assuming arbitrary values at the given set of prices of inputs subject only to the requirements of theoretical consistency' [Lau 1986]. In a flexible functional form it is possible to have variation in scale economies, capacity utilisation, substitution elasticities and technological bias across observations.

A difficult task for an empirical analyst is the choice among flexible functional forms. In production theory literature there are quite a few flexible functional forms, important ones being generalised Cobb-Douglas (GCD) [Diewert 1973], generalised Leontief (GL) [Diewert 1971], generalised square root quadratic (GSRQ) [Denny 1974], generalised Box-Cox (GBC) [Berndt and Khaled 1979], symmetric-generalized McFadden (SGM) [Diewert and Wales 1987] and translog (TL) [Christensen, Jorgenson and Lau 1971, 1973]. Many researchers have attempted comparative studies on the relative performance of flexible functional forms [see, for example, Applebaum 1979a; Berndt and Khaled 1979; Berndt, Darrough and Diewert 1977; Caves and Christensen 1980; Wales 1977 among others]. However, a consensus is not yet reached. Applebaum (1979a) and Park and Kwon (1995) prefer GL to TL form for explaining producer behaviour on the basis of better fit. On the other hand, Berndt, Darrough and Diewert (1977) conclude that TL is the preferred form. Wales (1977) finds that in certain cases GL performs better while in other cases it is TL. Berndt and Khaled (1979) adopt a generalised Box-Cox (GBC) form of which GL, TL and GSRQ are special cases. On the basis of empirical results they reject GSRQ, could not reject GL and found that tests on TL form were inconclusive.

In production theory literature the translog[17] functional form [Christensen, Jorgenson and Lau 1971, 1973] has been the most preferred functional form [Greene 1990]. Christensen, Jorgenson and Lau (1971) introduced the translog production frontier. By taking a single output as a special case Griliches and Ringstad (1971) and Sargan (1971) independently introduced the translog production function (as cited in Christensen *et al.* 1973). It is worth mentioning that translog cost function is not derived by any optimising procedure from the translog production function. Thus the translog has no self-dual. Rather the translog cost function is simply set up in the same way as the production function in terms of costs and prices rather than in terms of quantities. Thus the translog cost function does not imply a translog production function. However, both can be used if they are assumed to be second order approximations to the same underlying technology [Burgess 1975].

Specification of a Cost Function

There are three distinct specifications of a cost function depending upon relevant equilibrium conditions. These are: *(i)* long run total cost function pertaining to full static equilibrium (FSE) model; *(ii)* short-run restricted (variable) cost function resulting in partial static equilibrium (PSE) model; and *(iii)* restricted cost function with adjustment costs pertaining to partial dynamic equilibrium (PDE) models.

Full Static Equilibrium (FSE) Models

Early studies on productivity assumed all inputs to be variable so that the industry is under FSE. Some of the pioneering works on application of the FSE approach through the use of a translog cost function are Berndt and Wood (1975), Berndt and Christensen (1976) and Christensen and Greene (1976) among others. In mathematical notation, the FSE model is represented by

$$C = C(P_i, Y, t) \qquad \text{...(5.1)}$$

where P_i is input price, *Y* is output level and *t* is technology. Here all inputs are treated symmetrically and assumed to get adjusted to their long-run equilibrium level within one period of time [Kulatilaka 1985].

The assumption that all inputs are variable may not be a realistic depiction of the production process in situations where some of the inputs (e.g., capital and white collar labour) cannot be adjusted fully in the short-run but only in the long run. Quasi-fixity, i.e., fixed in short-run but variable in long-run, of these inputs gives rise to two different approaches: partial static and partial dynamic models.

Partial Static Equilibrium (PSE) Models

The PSE models are based on the distinction between the Marshallian notion of short-run and long-run equilibria. Here it is assumed that industry optimises over the variable inputs in the short-run given the quantity of quasi-fixed inputs [see Berndt and Fuss 1986; Berndt and Hesse 1986; Morrison 1988b & 1988c, among others]. The variable inputs adjust to their equilibrium level within a single period whereas the quasi-fixed input(s) adjust only partially. On the other hand, the quasi-fixed input can reach its equilibrium level only in the long-run. Such a specification implies that in the short-run as the industry cannot adjust its quasi-fixed factors to equilibrium levels there may be under-utilisation or over-utilisation of existing stock of the quasi-fixed factors depending upon market demand conditions.

In mathematical notation the PSE model is given by

$$VC = G(P, Y, K, t) \qquad \text{...(5.2)}$$

where VC is variable cost, P is a vector of variable inputs prices, K is a vector of quasi-fixed inputs quantities, Y is output and t is technology.

In PSE models variable and quasi-fixed inputs are treated asymmetrically in the sense that we take the prices of variable inputs and quantities of quasi-fixed inputs. The underlying logic is as follows: as K cannot be changed in the short-run, price of K does not influence its level. Rather the prime consideration before the industry is variable cost given the level of K. Thus, in the case of the short-run cost function[18] the level of the quasi-fixed inputs, instead of its price, enters as an argument into the cost function.

Partial Dynamic Equilibrium (PDE) Models

PDE models are formulated with the underlying logic that a higher level of investment can be undertaken only at a cost of lowering the current output level as new machinery installation disrupts the prevailing production arrangements. Thus there is an 'adjustment cost' involved in changing capital stock. Such an adjustment cost can be either internal or external to the firm. Internal adjustment cost, specific to the firm, may arise because *(i)* installation of new machinery disrupts the work routine of the labour force, *(ii)* the benefit of workers' learning-by-doing takes time, and *(iii)* the firm may be hesitant to undertake new investment with uncertain future demand as the investment process is irreversible [Hamermesh and Pfann 1996]. On the other hand, external adjustment cost arises in the form of increased financing cost and competition within the industry [Pindyck and Rotemberg 1983].

In case adjustment costs are internal to the firm the variable cost function is specified with rate of change in quasi-fixed input as one of the arguments [Morrison 1988c; Park and Kwon 1995] which increases the number of parameters to be estimated. External adjustment costs[19] are introduced as separate equations into the model [Epstein and Denny 1980; Nadiri and Kim 1996; Pindyck and Rotemberg 1983].

Thus PDE models with internal adjustment cost can be given by the following notation:

$$VC = G(P, Y, K, \dot{K}, t) \qquad ...(5.3)$$

where $\dot{K}$ is a vector of the rate of change in quasi-fixed inputs.

On the other hand, PDE model with external adjustment costs is given by the joint function

$$VC = G(P,Y,K,t), \text{ and}$$

$$C' = I(\dot{K}) \qquad ...(5.4)$$

where C' is a convex function in $\dot{K}$, which implies that adjustment costs cannot be negative.

In PDE models the industry confronts an inter-temporal cost minimisation problem so as to yield explicit time paths for fixed inputs. A simpler variant of dynamic models, namely, partial dynamic models, does not set explicit time paths for quasi-fixed inputs but uses Euler equations in solving the dynamic problems [see Berndt, Morrison and Watkins 1979; Morrison 1992; Park and Kwon 1995; Pindyck and Rotemberg 1983; Nadiri and Kim 1996 among others]. Thus, from the perspective of empirical estimation, the difference between PSE and PDE models is the 'Euler equation', which is added to the cost and variable factor demand equations in the case of PDE formulation.

It was a study by Berndt, Morrison and Watkins (1979) which first estimated factor demand equations by combining the developments in duality theory with the adjustment costs model. Some of the limitations of their model such as exogeneity of output and linear variable factor demand equations [McIntosh 1982] were removed later [see Morrison 1992; Morrison and Berndt 1981; and Park and Kwon 1995 among others]. Some of the important studies based on internal adjustment costs are Morrison (1986, 1988a, 1992), Park and Kwon (1995) and Epstein and Denny (1980) while external adjustment costs are dealt with in Pindyck and Rotemberg (1983) and Nadiri and Kim (1996), among others.

Choice among the Three Specifications

While early literature on productivity assumed FSE for describing producer behaviour, recent studies have made use of either PSE or PDE models. In fact, some inputs, particularly capital and white-collar labour, seem to be accepted as quasi-fixed inputs more frequently than as variable ones. There are quite a few studies which have delved into the problem of testing for whether production takes place under full static or partial static equilibrium [Aitkinson and Halvorsen 1998; Hazilla and Kopp 1986; Kulatilaka 1985; Schankerman and Nadiri 1986]. These studies conclude that capital can be taken as a quasi-fixed input but labour may not. For example, Morrison (1988a) infers that labour may not be a quasi-fixed input in the case of U.S. and Japan aggregate manufacturing industries. Such an inference is on the basis of higher R-squared values reported in alternative specifications. Pindyck and Rotemberg (1983) conclude that labour is a variable input in the U.S. aggregate manufacturing industries, as they find the adjustment cost of labour to be negligible.

It is useful to point out that in the case of Indian manufacturing industries, Srivastava (1996) takes labour as a quasi-fixed input along with capital on the ground that Indian labour laws are stringent in hiring and firing of labour. However, a major chunk of the labour force in Indian industries is in the form of casual or contract labour, so that its size can be adjusted even in the short-run.

The choice between PSE and PDE models is a difficult one. According to Kulatilaka (1985) the PSE model does not explicitly treat the adjustment path from the short-run to the long-run. Thus, it does not specify *(i)* how long it takes for the quasi-fixed input to reach its equilibrium level, *(ii)* what inter-temporal path it takes, and *(iii)* what criteria are used in determining the adjustment path. Notwithstanding such observations, the PSE model is preferred to the PDE model because of the following disadvantages associated with the latter.

First, PDE models are not only difficult to implement empirically but also may not hold in situations when disequilibrium in a quasi-fixed factor is due to non-market factors [Brown and Christensen 1981]. For example, in a regulatory regime capital may not be fully mobile and may not reach its equilibrium level even in the long-run. The fact that the Indian paper industry has operated most of the time in a regulated policy regime suggests that PSE may be more appropriate than PDE.

Second, in the case of the translog formulation incorporation of internal adjustment cost is difficult as the specification of Euler equations for quasi-fixed inputs requires second-order derivatives, which is quite complex to derive and difficult to implement in empirical models. In order to reduce complexities some researchers [Nadiri and Kim 1996; Pindyck and Rotemberg 1983] have assumed adjustment cost to be external to the industry. However, according to Morrison (1988a) external adjustment costs are much less compared to internal adjustment costs.

Third, the assumption of a smooth convex symmetric external adjustment costs function rules out potentially interesting asymmetries regarding adjustment costs and disinvestment [Schankerman and Nadiri 1986]. Thus the translog variable cost function with symmetric external adjustment cost may not be a preferred choice.

Fourth, according to Nemoto, Nakanishi and Madano (1993) the PSE model has the advantage of unspecified capital adjustment remaining compatible with whatever path capital is adjusted along.

TFP Estimation Procedures in Indian Studies

Productivity studies in India have followed all three approaches (index number, econometric and non-parametric) discussed above. While the index number approach has been used by most of the studies [Ahluwalia 1985 & 1991; Balakrishnan and Pushpangadan 1994; Banerjee 1975; Brahmananda 1982; Dholakia and Dholakia 1994; Goldar 1986; Pradhan and Barik 1998; Rao 1996; Srivastava 1996], some of the studies have attempted econometric estimation [Ahluwalia 1991; Apte 1983; Basant and Fikkert 1996; Bhavani 1991a; Bharadwaj 1994; Gangopadhyaya and Wadhwa 1998; Jha, Murty and Paul 1991; Jha, Murty, Paul and Rao 1993; Panda 1998; Pradhan and Barik 1999a & 1999b; Srivastava 1996]. The non-parametric approach[20] has been adopted in Majumdar (1996). The studies of Bhavani (1991b), Bharadwaj (1994), Goldar (1985), Jha, Murty and Sahni (1992) and Mitra (1999) estimate technical efficiency compared to the best practice firm by means of decomposing the error components from estimates of a parametric model.

Most of the studies are based on the translog index (Divisia-Tornquist approximation) with the exception of Brahmananda (1982) which is based solely on the Kendrick index for analysis. Ahluwalia (1985 &1991) and Goldar (1986) use the translog index for analysis but estimate Kendrick and Solow indices respectively to reinforce their results.

Studies Based on Index Number Approach

Studies based on the index number approach and using the translog index can be divided into two categories according to the output variable considered—gross value added or gross output. Some studies [Pradhan and Barik 1998; Rao 1996; Srivastava 1996] have taken value of gross output adjusted for price changes as a measure of output to be explained by capital, labour and intermediate inputs. On the other hand, the studies of Ahluwalia (1985 & 1991), Balakrishnan and Pushpangadan (1994), Banerjee (1975), Brahmananda (1982), Dholakia and Dholakia (1994) and Goldar (1986) have taken gross value added as a measure of output while estimating TFP.

Within the group of studies attempting an index number approach to TFP estimation and taking value added as a measure of output, there are two different strands based on obtaining value added either by single deflation [Ahluwalia 1985 & 1991; Goldar 1986] or by double deflation [Balakrishnan and Pushpangadan 1994; Dholakia and Dholakia 1994]. Gross value added (GVA) provided in official statistics of India is obtained by subtracting the value of intermediate inputs from the value of gross output at current prices. GVA so obtained is adjusted for price changes by wholesale price index of output. Such a procedure is termed single deflation as both output and intermediate inputs are deflated by the same index. GVA by double deflation, on the other hand, is obtained by subtracting intermediate inputs deflated by their price index from gross output deflated by a price index of output [Bruno 1984]. So long as growth rates in prices of gross output and intermediate inputs are more or less the same both measures yield identical estimates. However, if output prices increase at a rate different from intermediate input the single deflation method involves serious bias in representing the true growth rate in TFP [Balakrishnan and Pushpangadan 1994]. As the ratio of output to intermediate input prices has not remained constant in India Balakrishnan and Pushpangadan (1994) suggest the adoption of gross value added with double deflation as a measure of output.

The two variants of TFP estimation from GVA produce different results for the same set of data. In the case of the aggregate manufacturing sector of India, Ahluwalia (1991) and Balakrishnan and Pushpangadan (1994) have obtained quite contrasting results. While the study by Balakrishnan and Pushpangadan (1994) found a statistically significant negative trend in the growth rate of TFP on application of the double deflation method, Ahluwalia's (1991) use of the single deflation method provided a statistically significant positive trend.

A crucial factor in empirical implementation of the double deflation method is the price index of raw material. Balakrishnan and Pushpangadan (1994), Goldar (2000), Pradhan and Barik (1998), Rao (1996) and Trivedi *et al.* (2000) make use of the economy-wide Input-Output table to construct a materials input index. Such a procedure is criticised by Dholakia and Dholakia (1994) on the ground that only an Input-Output table covering the registered manufacturing sector would provide an appropriate material price index[21].

The use of value added as a proxy for output has the advantage that it avoids the problem of double counting. Secondly, in industries where production processes are vertically integrated (that is, output at one stage is used as input in the next), higher productivity in one stage may get averaged with low productivity in the later ones. Nonetheless use of value added in place of output is valid only if intermediate inputs are separable from primary inputs. According to Sargent (1992) the use of gross output in contrast to value added can be justified in any situation. In practice firms produce output, not value added, and take production decisions with some discretion on the intermediate input level as on labour and capital.

Rao (1996) points out that a bias is involved in adopting value added as a measure of output whether it is obtained by single or double discounting and suggests use of gross output instead. It has been observed that Indian industries do not fulfill separability conditions [Bhavani 1991a; Pradhan and Barik 1998; Williams and Lauma 1981]. Hence Balakrishnan and Pushpangadan (1998) re-emphasize that unless the separability condition is met productivity studies should take gross output as a measure of output.

A major limitation of the index number approach is that it restricts technology to yield constant returns to scale, as mentioned earlier. The growth rate in TFP obtained through such a method is adjusted for non-constant returns to scale and product market imperfection [Denny, Fuss and Waverman 1981]. However, studies in TFP of Indian manufacturing industries have not attempted such adjustments although the presence of non-constant returns to scale is indicated [see, for example, Jha, Murty and Paul 1991; Jha, Murty, Paul and Rao 1993]. In the case of the paper industry also the presence of diseconomies of scale is indicated by Pradhan and Barik (1999b).

Studies Based on Econometric Approach

The second strand of studies are based on econometric estimation [Ahluwalia 1991; Bhavani 1991a; Bharadwaj 1994; Gangopadhyaya and Wadhwa 1998; Jha, Murty and Paul 1991; Jha, Murty, Paul and Rao 1993; Panda 1998; Pradhan and Barik 1999a and 1999b; Srivastava 1996] of production or cost function in Indian industries. These studies can be divided into three broad groups, viz., *(i)* those based on gross value added [Ahluwalia 1991; Gangopadhyaya and Wadhwa 1998], *(ii)* those based on gross output (or its dual cost) but adopting a FSE framework [Bhavani 1991a; Panda 1998; Pradhan and Barik 1999a and 1999b], and *(iii)* those based on a PSE model [Bharadwaj 1994; Srivastava 1996 and 2000]. Of these studies, some have covered the manufacturing sector [Ahluwalia 1991; Gangopadhyaya and Wadhwa 1998; Pradhan and Barik 1999a and 1999b; Srivastava 1996 and 2000] while others are industry specific [Bhavani 1991a; Panda 1998; Bharadwaj 1994]. Secondly, the studies of Ahluwalia (1991), Bhavani (1991a), Gangopadhyaya and Wadhwa (1998), Pradhan and Barik (1999a and 1999b) are based on aggregate industry level data while those of Bharadwaj (1994), Panda (1998) and Srivastava (1996 &2000) have used firm level data.

The specific-industry based firm-level studies [Bharadwaj

1994; Panda 1998] have the advantage of explaining firm-level variations in productivity and identifying best practice firms. Bharadwaj (1994) takes into account four major steel producing plants in India and makes a comparative analysis of their productivity performance. Similarly, Panda (1998) takes into account the road transport vehicle industry in India, which mainly consists of seven firms. However, analysis at a firm level is suitable if the industry is oligopolistic with a limited number of firms. In the case of industries with a large number of units, firm level comparison may not be of much use. In line with this reasoning, Srivastava (1996 and 2000) presents a comparative analysis at the industry level even though estimation is made with firm level data.

The lacunae arising out of the earlier mentioned non-fulfilment of separability conditions between primary and intermediate inputs applies to the studies of Ahluwalia (1991) and Gangopadhyaya and Wadhwa (1998). Some of the studies [for example, Jha, Murty and Paul 1991; Jha and Sahni 1991] have taken a truncated version of the translog cost function implying autonomous technological progress to be zero. In these studies scope for technological bias is provided but technological progress over time is not allowed. Such a limitation, however, is removed in Jha, Murty, Paul and Rao (1993) and a translog cost function with all relevant parameters is estimated.

Another issue with the TFP estimation in India is concerning the estimation procedure of the translog production (cost) function. It is worth mentioning that factor demand equations[22] can be derived from a translog cost function by taking logarithmic differentiation and applying Shephard's lemma [Shephard 1953]. Ahluwalia (1991) while estimating translog value added function and Bhavani (1991a) while estimating a translog production function do not take into account the share equations on the ground of large number of observations. Such a procedure is likely to provide consistent and unbiased, but inefficient, estimates as has been mentioned by Christensen and Greene (1976).

Econometric estimation of a translog production (cost) function requires estimation of a large number of parameters and hence, a larger data set. The number of parameters to be estimated increases with the number of inputs. In order to keep the problem manageable some of the studies have restricted the number of inputs to three, viz., capital (*K*), labour (*L*), and energy and raw materials (*EM*) [Jha, Murty and Paul 1991]. However, Jha, Murty, Paul and Rao (1993) specify a translog cost function with four inputs (*K, L, E, M*) while analysing scale economies, factor substitution and biased technological change in four selected Indian manufacturing industries. The paper industry being energy intensive, energy (*E*) needs to be considered as a separate input instead of being grouped together with materials input (*M*).

Limitations in Indian Studies

The preceding discussion points out quite a few limitations of the productivity studies undertaken for Indian manufacturing industries. The index number approach provides an estimate of TFP, which reflects technological progress under CRTS, full capacity utilisation and perfect competition in the product market. When these conditions are not met, TFP tends to be a biased estimate of technological change.

Some of the factors, such as non-constant returns to scale, presence of market power and non-constant utilisation of capacity, can be isolated through econometric estimation of a cost function. Accordingly the Solow residual can be adjusted for these factors so as to obtain a realistic estimate of technological change in the industry.

In the analysis of productivity growth of the Indian paper industry, which is pursued in the present study, we attempt to relax the above mentioned assumptions. First, we take the route of employing a flexible translog cost function in our econometric estimation which allows us to simultaneous estimation of scale economies, capacity utilisation and mark-up in the industry. Second, our assumption of a partial static equilibrium framework enables us to take capital as a quasi-fixed input such that it reaches its equilibrium level only in the long-run. Third, we allow mark-up in product pricing, instead of the usual assumption of perfect competition in the industry. Such a formulation provides scope for relaxing the stringent assumptions of the index number approach. Finally, in order to have a realistic estimate of technological change in the industry we adjust the traditional productivity growth obtained through Divisia-Tornquist approximation for non-fulfilment of the standard assumptions underlying the index number approach such as non-constant returns to scale, under-utilisation of capacity and mark-up.

Notes

1. According to Diewert (1980) there are four approaches to productivity measurement, viz., *(i)* index number, *(ii)* Divisia, *(iii)* econometric, and *(iv)* non-parametric. Commenting on this, Christensen (1980) suggests that the first two approaches are almost similar and hence can be combined into one, that is index number approach.
2. The non-parametric approach is more appropriate with firm-level data. Since the present study deals with the issue at an aggregate industry level such an approach is presumed to be inappropriate. Therefore, review of the non-parametric approach followed in productivity analysis is not given here despite the existence of a vast literature in the area (see, for example, Bauer 1990; Forsund, Lovell and Schmidt 1980; Greene 1997).
3. See Diewert (1980) for a comprehensive presentation of the comparative merits and demerits of these methods.
4. If $TFP = \frac{Y}{X}$ where Y is output and X is weighted inputs then $\dot{TFP} = \dot{Y} - \dot{X}$ where 'dot' over a variable indicates the concerned growth rate. It is not difficult to see that growth rate in TFP thus obtained is a residual. It was Solow (1957) who first formulated such an equation through a neo-classical production function. In due recognition of his pioneering efforts it is often termed as the 'Solow residual'.
5. In the presence of more than one output, a similarly weighted index of output also is required.
6. Diewert (1976) suggests two additional desirable properties. These are: one, if an index can be derived from some underlying utility, production, cost or revenue function this index can be called 'exact' and two, if the underlying production or utility function is flexible the index can be called 'superlative' [Good, Nadiri and Sickles 1997].
7. Therefore, the Kendrick index is given by $A_t = \frac{Y_t}{w_0 L_t + r_0 K_t}$ where *A* is productivity, *Y, L, K* are output, labour and capital respectively, *w* and *r* are returns to labour and capital respectively.

8. The equation for the Solow index is $\frac{\Delta A}{A}=\frac{\Delta Y}{Y}-\left(S_K\frac{\Delta K}{K}+S_L\frac{\Delta L}{L}\right)$ where S_K and S_L are income shares of capital and labour respectively.
9. For discrete data it is obtained by the Divisia-Tornquist approximation. Diewert (1976) has shown that the Divisia-Tornquist approximation to TFP is exact if the underlying production function is translog.
10. Homogeneous input quality may not be a realistic assumption in many cases. In fact 'learning by doing' may improve labour quality over time and thereby increase labour productivity. Similarly technological progress may result in better quality capital inputs. Hence it is highly debatable whether technological progress is embodied in inputs, particularly in capital, or is 'disembodied' [see, for example, Denison 1964; Hall 1968; Hercowitz 1998; Hulten 1992]. One basic assumption of the embodiment hypothesis is that productivity of new capital is higher than that of older capital. However, Denison (1964) considered such a hypothesis to be not important, as age distribution of capital stock has a small impact on output growth. On the other hand, protagonists of the disembodiment hypothesis hold the view that capital stock of different vintages differs only by some fixed factor associated with depreciation and retirement of capital. The rate of depreciation (δ) converts each vintage of investment into new-machine equivalents. Thus the stock of capital at time *t*, *K(t)*, can be interpreted as the number of new-machine equivalents implied by past investments [Hulten 1992]. The present study confines itself to disembodied technological change keeping in view the following two points: the methodology of disembodied technological progress offers wide scope for analysing production structure and the data requirement for modeling embodied technological progress is quite demanding.
11. Hicks-neutral technological change implies that factor ratios do not change when factor prices remain unchanged. Technological change is said to be Hicks-neutral if at constant capital labour ratio the marginal rate of substitution stays constant, that is, $\frac{d}{dt}MRS=\frac{d}{dt}\frac{MP_K}{MP_L}=-\frac{d}{dt}\frac{dL}{dK}=0$ [Binswanger 1974]. Hicks-neutrality is different from Harrod-neutrality where the capital-output ratio remains unchanged if price of capital is constant and Solow-neutrality where the labour-output ratio remains unchanged if labour price remain constant. Thus input shares are assumed

to remain constant over time in the case of Hicks-neutrality [Nadiri 1982].

12. The price possibility frontier (PPF) was introduced by Samuelson (1953). For a single output and many inputs Samuelson referred to PPF as factor-price frontier. For formulation of the translog price function and its properties see Jorgenson (1986).
13. As we observed in Chapter 2, use of a cost function allows for non-constant returns to scale, mark-up and under-utilisation of capacity.
14. The elements of a Hessian matrix indicate elasticities of substitution. For twice differentiable technology the Hessian matrix is symmetric. Thus with n inputs, it has n diagonal and $\frac{1}{2}n(n-1)$ off-diagonal elements.
15. For example, this class of production functions restricts the elasticity of substitution between inputs. In the case of a Cobb-Douglas production function the elasticity of substitution between inputs is constrained to unity whereas in CES it is a specified constant.
16. It can be derived as either differential approximation (particularly Taylor's series) or numerical approximation of the second order to any arbitrary function. [See Chambers 1988 for details]. Some researchers have attempted a third-order approximation to the translog function [see, for example, Stevenson 1980]. Such an approach, however, has not been popular because of difficulties in interpretation of parameters and loss of degree of freedom due to introduction of additional parameters.
17. It stands for transcendental logarithmic. The word transcendental in mathematical parlance means something which is not algebraic. In translog form both the dependent and independent variables are in logarithmic terms.
18. Also called variable cost function which is a special case of variable profit function. According to Brown and Christensen (1981) the first empirical application of a variable profit function appears to be Lau and Yotopoulos (1971).
19. There are a variety of forms for adjustment costs of which four are prominent, viz., *(i)* symmetric convex (quadratic), *(ii)* asymmetric convex, *(iii)* piecewise linear, and *(iv)* lumpy costs [Hamermesh and Pfann 1996]. Of these, symmetric quadratic is used in aggregative productivity studies frequently because of its simple formulation and it can embody rational expectations [for example, Pindyck and Rotemberg 1983].

20. As mentioned earlier non-parametric approach is more appropriate with firm-level data. Since the present study deals the issues at an aggregate industry level non-parametric approach is not pursued. Concurrently, review of the non-parametric approach followed in productivity studies on Indian industries is not given here.
21. Detailed discussion of the construction of the materials input price index and its limitations are given in Chapter 3.
22. Results take the form of share equations for the variable inputs. See Chapter 2 for details.

6

Productivity Growth: Preliminary Results

Keeping in view the fact that the index number approach provides a good testing ground for assessment of productivity growth, we estimate partial factor productivity (PFP) and total factor productivity (TFP) for the Indian paper industry. We begin with the partial productivity for individual inputs after which estimates of TFP for the Indian paper industry are given.

Partial Productivity of Inputs

In order to ascertain the efficiency with which individual inputs are utilised in the production process we computed partial productivity indexes of all the inputs. It is useful to point out that partial productivity is derived for an input and is given by the ratio of total output to input concerned. Thus partial productivity reflects the pattern of changes in the average product of the input under consideration. Traditionally labour productivity has been recognised as a measure of efficiency with which labour input is used in the production process. However, partial productivity of other inputs can also be derived in a similar manner, in order to gain insight on their utilisation.

We estimate partial productivity indexes for capital, labour, energy and material for the paper industry over the period 1973-74 to 1997-98. The results are presented in Table 6.1 and plotted against time in Fig. 6.1.

It is seen from Table 6.1 that labour productivity in the industry has gone up in contrast to partial productivity of other inputs. The increase in labour productivity could arise out of two possibilities, viz., qualitative improvement in labour input and increase in the level of accompanying factors per worker, particularly capital. Since the present study starts with a basic premise of homogeneous input quality, an analysis of qualitative changes in labour input is not envisaged at the moment.

Table 6.1
Partial Productivity Indexes of Inputs: 1973-98

Year	*Partial Productivity of*			
	K	*L*	*E*	*M*
1973-74	100.00	100.00	100.00	100.00
1974-75	82.45	87.51	92.47	105.77
1975-76	97.05	104.53	101.56	110.77
1976-77	96.92	107.19	100.70	110.06
1977-78	100.21	106.87	88.70	106.98
1978-79	98.31	110.14	91.50	103.45
1979-80	100.90	107.73	85.99	101.60
1980-81	92.57	110.94	89.08	104.05
1981-82	104.00	127.72	98.94	115.57
1982-83	78.17	97.28	76.78	96.78
1983-84	75.53	112.71	75.30	97.71
1984-85	79.27	138.24	75.18	98.23
1985-86	87.98	136.95	72.83	89.07
1986-87	82.67	145.99	70.47	93.46
1987-88	76.86	138.66	64.66	89.50
1988-89	75.95	158.01	66.73	89.37
1989-90	95.50	181.99	67.18	88.75
1990-91	95.37	194.70	75.06	88.47
1991-92	86.73	180.53	64.42	87.06
1992-93	76.36	158.29	59.52	84.38
1993-94	74.49	166.63	69.75	86.22
1994-95	64.83	201.16	74.69	89.47
1995-96	88.39	217.15	71.50	89.12
1996-97	75.56	213.29	67.82	86.60
1997-98	81.82	209.20	80.56	86.63

In order to examine the role of accompanying factors in the improvement of labour productivity, we computed the capital-labour ratio in the industry. We found the ratio of capital stock (at 1981-82 prices) to total persons engaged in the industry. In order to have a sharper analysis on the direction of the capital-labour ratio we normalised it for the beginning year. As a result, we found that the capital-labour ratio in the industry increased from 100 in 1973-74 to 255.68 in 1997-98 (see Fig. 6.2 which plots the capital-labour ratio against time). Thus labour is being utilised with increasing amount of capital which is increasing its efficiency.

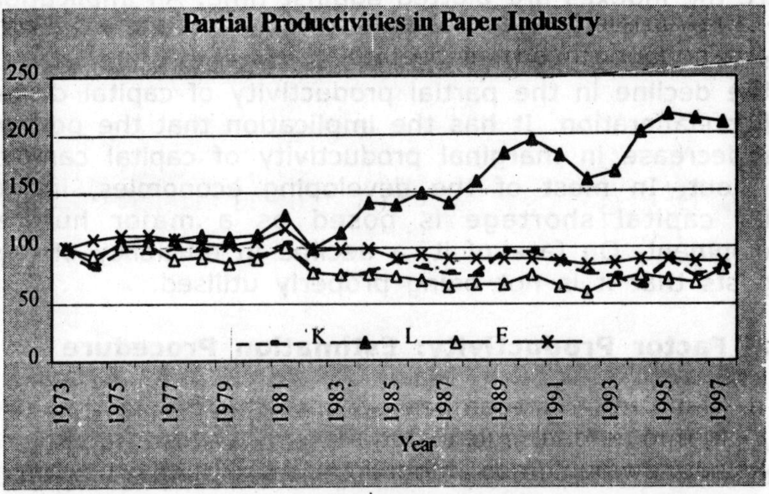

Fig. 6.1

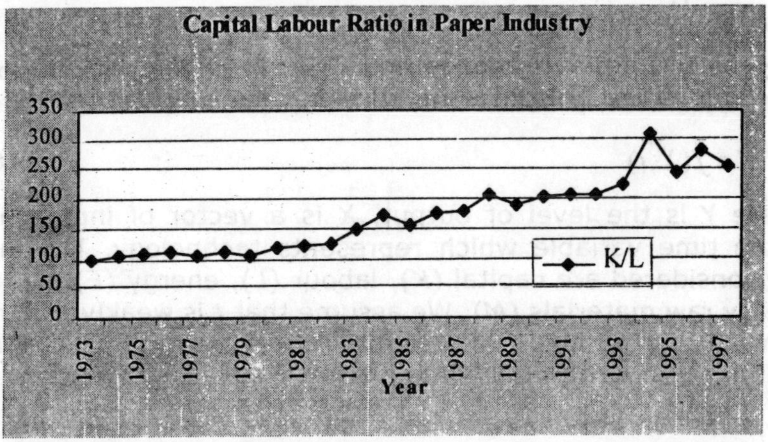

Fig. 6.2

In contrast to the observed increase in labour productivity, the decrease in partial productivity of capital, energy and raw material is a distinct feature of the industry. Starting from a productivity level of 100 in the year 1973-74, the partial productivity indexes for capital, energy and raw material have declined to 81.82, 80.56 and 86.63 respectively (see Table 6.1). Such declines in the partial productivity of capital, energy and raw material are shown more clearly in Fig. 6.1 where the indexes are plotted against time. An implication of the declines is that the efficiency with which these inputs are utilised in the production process is declining over time.

The decline in the partial productivity of capital deserves further elaboration. It has the implication that the possibility of a decrease in marginal productivity of capital cannot be ruled out. In most of the developing economies, including India, capital shortage is posed as a major hurdle to development. On face of it, a decline in efficiency of capital suggests that it is not being properly utilised.

Total Factor Productivity: Estimation Procedure

We estimate TFP residually by subtracting the growth rate in inputs from that of output. For obtaining the growth rate in all inputs combined we take a Divisia index of inputs. As discrete data at annual intervals are used, we take a Divisia-Tornquist approximation for obtaining growth rates in TFP.

Divisia-Tornquist Approximation

In order to derive the Divisia-Tornquist approximation we begin with an arbitrary twice differentiable production function[1]:

$$Y = f(X,t) \qquad \text{...(6.1)}$$

where Y is the level of output, X is a vector of inputs and t is the time variable which represents technology. The inputs (X_i) considered are capital (K), labour (L), energy (E) and non-energy raw materials (M). We assume that t is weakly separable from X which implies that technological change is Hicks-neutral. By taking logarithmic differentiation of (6.1) we obtain

$$\frac{d\ln Y}{dt} = \sum_i \frac{\partial \ln f}{\partial \ln X_i}\frac{\partial \ln X_i}{\partial t} + \frac{\partial \ln f}{\partial t} \quad (i \text{ represents input}) \quad ...(6.2)$$

$$\dot{Y} = \sum_i \varepsilon_{Yi}\, \dot{X}_i + TFP$$

where $\varepsilon_{Yi} = \dfrac{\partial \ln f}{\partial \ln X_i}$ is the elasticity of output with respect to X_i;

$\dot{TFP} = \dfrac{\partial \ 1n\ f}{\partial t}$ is the growth rate in TFP; a dot over a variable represents the growth rate in it. On re-arranging terms in the above we get

$$\dot{TFP} = \dot{Y} - \sum_i \varepsilon_{Yi}\dot{X}_i \quad ...(6.3)$$

Estimating the growth rate of TFP from (6.3) could have been straightforward if we had appropriate values for output elasticities, ε_{Yi}. However, we do not have realistic measure of ε_{Yi}, particularly ε_{YK}, the output elasticity of capital, because *(i)* capital input is durable in the sense that it does not get completely exhausted in a single use, and *(ii)* a perfect market does not exist for capital input. Thus what enters into the production process are the services of the capital stock which are difficult to measure. Even if we assume that capital services are proportional to its stock, in the absence of a perfect market for capital input we cannot ascertain its market rental price. The contribution of capital to output at the margin, which is essential in empirical measurement of input elasticity, is thus not observed. This requires us to make further assumptions on technology. In order to simplify the issue we assume that the production function exhibits constant returns to scale (CRTS) and each factor is paid according to its marginal product. Under these assumptions the first order condition of equilibrium of a firm is given by

$$\frac{\partial f}{\partial X_i} = \frac{P_i}{P_Y}$$

where P_i is the price of X_i and P_Y is the price of output *Y*. On application of Euler's product exhaustion theorem we find that the payment to capital is the residual after other factor rewards are taken into account. Given such a condition, (6.2) can be written as

$$\frac{d\ln Y}{dt} = \sum_i \frac{\partial f}{\partial X_i}\frac{X_i}{Y}\frac{\partial \ln X_i}{\partial t} + \frac{\partial \ln f}{\partial t}$$

or, $$\frac{d\ln Y}{dt} = \sum_i \frac{P_i X_i}{P_Y Y}\frac{\partial \ln X_i}{\partial t} + \frac{\partial \ln f}{\partial t}$$

or, $$\dot{TFP} = \dot{Y} - \sum_i s_i \dot{X}_i \qquad ...(6.4)$$

where $s_i = \dfrac{P_i X_i}{P_Y Y}$ is the expenditure share of the ith input in revenue.

It may be noted that in (6.4) the factor shares are given in current prices, as in $s_i = \dfrac{P_i X_i}{P_Y Y}$. The numerator ($P_i X_i$) is expenditure on the ith input while the denominator ($P_Y Y$) is revenue of the firm or industry. Thus the factor shares used in the equation are at current prices. Secondly, the share of capital is obtained by subtracting factor shares of labour, energy and material inputs from unity, that is,

$$s_K = 1 - s_L - s_E - s_M$$

It may be noted that the second term on the right hand side of (6.4) is the proportionate change in Divisia index of inputs.

Implementation of (6.4) empirically requires growth rates in inputs and output, and factor shares in revenue (or in cost, as cost = revenue in long-run equilibrium in a perfectly competitive product market). However, a major limitation of such a formulation is that data are not available on a continuous basis. Hence, for discrete data we need to have some approximation to (6.4). We take resort to the Divisia-Tornquist approximation where, for two periods of time, *t* and *t-1*, s_i

is approximated by the average of shares in both periods, and growth rates are the logarithmic difference. In equation form the Divisia-Tornquist approximation is given by[2]

$$\dot{TFP} = (\ln Y_t - \ln Y_{t-1}) - \frac{1}{2}\sum_i (s_{i,t} + s_{i,t-1})(\ln X_{i,t} - \ln X_{i,t-1}) \quad ...(6.5)$$

$$(i = K, L, E, M)$$

where $X_{i,t}$ denotes the ith input for the tth year and $s_{i,t}$ is the share of ith input in revenue for the tth year.

While estimating $\dot{TFP}$ in (6.5) we include intermediate inputs (*E* and *M*) in addition to primary inputs (*K, L*) as arguments of the production function and take gross output (instead of value added) as a measure of output. This is for two reasons: one, according to a study [Pradhan and Barik 1998] the Indian paper industry does not fulfil the condition that primary inputs are separable from intermediate inputs. Two, taking value added as a measure of output and excluding intermediate inputs would not be consistent with the translog cost function used in the study.

Trend Growth in TFP

Growth rates in TFP that we obtain through (6.5) are on an annual basis and thus are expected to show fluctuation from year to year. From the annual growth rates in TFP we construct an index of TFP such that

$$TFP_t = TFP_{t-1} \exp(\dot{TFP}_{t-1}) \quad ...(6.6)$$

where TFP_t is the productivity index for period *t* and $\dot{TFP}_t$ is its growth rate for period *t*. We obtain a time series of the productivity index by implementing (6.6) which is amenable to further analysis. By using this index we estimate the trend growth rate in TFP by fitting a semi-log equation, which takes the form

$$\ln TFP_t = \theta_1 + \theta_2 t + \varepsilon_t \quad ...(6.7)$$

where *t* represents time and ε is the error term. From (6.7) the trend growth rate in TFP is obtained by taking ($e^{\theta_2} - 1$).

In order to examine possible structural breaks in the TFP index obtained in (6.6) we fit a linear spline function [Poirier 1974] which provides variable growth rates across sub-periods. A major problem with ascertaining structural breaks is our ignorance of the break points. In order to have a basis for identifying structural breaks we take recourse to CUSUM squared and sequential-Chow tests [Greene 1990]. On confirmation of structural breaks on the basis of the above-mentioned tests, the time series of the TFP index is divided into sub-periods. It is assumed that each sub-period has a uniform growth rate, which may be different from others. A spline function[3] [Poirier 1974; Greene 1990] is fitted to the natural logarithm of the TFP index, which provides variable growth rates across sub-periods.

Estimates of TFP

On the basis of Divisia-Tornquist approximation we estimated the annual growth rates in TFP of the Indian paper industry over the period 1973-74 to 1997-98. From such growth rates we obtained a TFP index across years which is presented in Table 6.2. Analysis of the index series provides us with two major observations:

First, the Indian paper industry is beset with negative productivity growth during the period of study. It is seen from Table 6.2 that the TFP index witnessed a decline from 100 in the year 1973-74 to 92.06 in 1997-98[4]. This has a serious implication for the long-run viability of the industry as well as efficient utilisation of scarce resources available in the economy. It can be inferred from the table that over time the input requirement per unit of output in the industry has increased. Again, the Indian paper industry has not been able to utilise its resources efficiently, and such inefficiency is increasing over time.

Second, the decline in TFP has not been consistent and there have been variations in its level. It is seen from Table 6.2 that the industry reached its highest level of productivity in 1981-82 with a level of 112.0 while in the year 1992-93 it witnessed a trough (83.09). The pattern of movement in the TFP level is better appreciated when it is plotted against time (see Fig. 6.3). It is observed from the figure that the TFP index remained above 100 up to the year 1981-82 (except for 1974-75) after which the declining phase set in.

Table 6.2
TFP Index in Paper Industry: 1973-98

Year	*TFP*	*Year*	*TFP*
1973-74	100	1986-87	91.20
1974-75	95.11	1987-88	86.10
1975-76	105.33	1988-89	87.21
1976-77	105.15	1989-90	92.80
1977-78	103.14	1990-91	94.54
1978-79	101.66	1991-92	89.00
1979-80	100.43	1992-93	83.09
1980-81	100.15	1993-94	85.99
1981-82	112.00	1994-95	86.67
1982-83	89.37	1995-96	93,82
1983-84	90.31	1996-97	88.01
1984-85	93.28	1997-98	92.06
1985-86	89.97	—	—

Note: TFP index is obtained from Divisia-Tornquist approximation on the basis of equation (6.6). Values are rounded off to two decimal places.

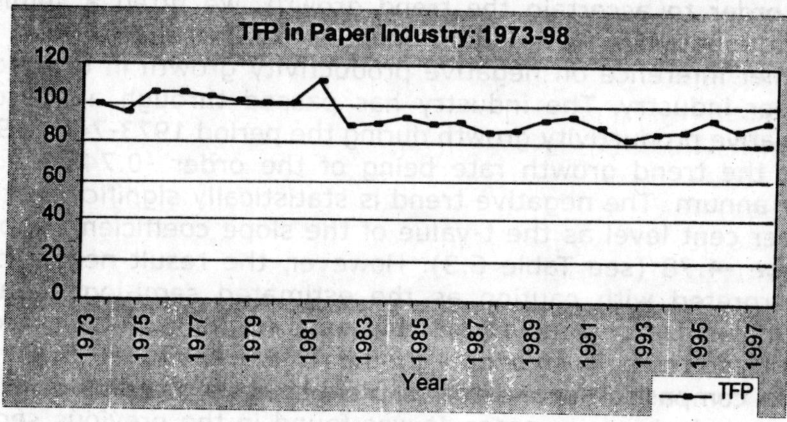

Fig. 6.3

Apart from the above two observations, another can be

added on the fluctuations in productivity level. By plotting the annual growth rates in TFP over time (see Fig. 6.4) we notice that there are local peaks and troughs in the productivity level throughout the study period. In the presence of such fluctuations it is difficult to draw any meaningful inference on the long-run growth path of TFP in the industry.

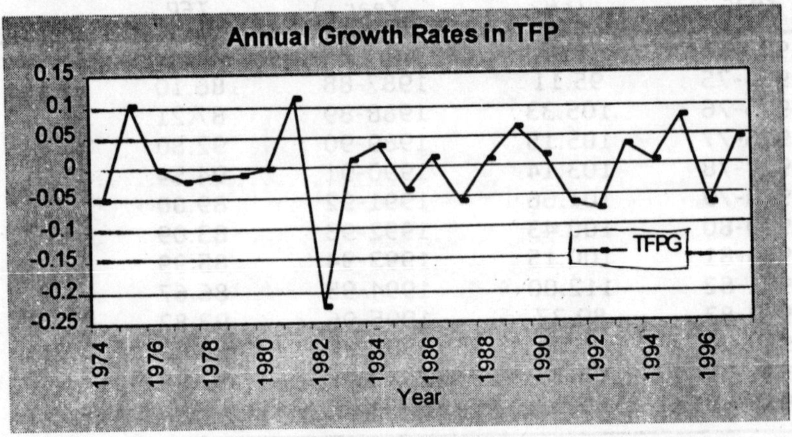

Fig. 6.4

Trend Growth in TFP

In order to ascertain the trend growth, we fitted a semi-log equation to the TFP index. Such an exercise confirmed our earlier inference on negative productivity growth in the Indian paper industry. The industry has passed through a phase of negative productivity growth during the period 1973-74 to 1997-98, the trend growth rate being of the order -0.74 per cent per annum. The negative trend is statistically significant at the 1 per cent level as the t-value of the slope coefficient is found to be -4.78 (see Table 6.3). However, the result needs to be interpreted with caution as the estimated semi-log equation indicated a moderate fit, with R-squared at 0.50, which could be ascribed to fluctuations in the TFP level.

A comparison of the partial productivities with TFP in Indian paper industry is in order. It was found in the previous section that productivity of capital, energy and raw material in the industry has decreased during the period of study (see Table

6.1). The industry has experienced an increase in labour productivity only. However, keeping in view the fact that TFP is a more comprehensive measure than PFP, the trend exhibited by TFP is more appropriate for the industry. This brings home the point that productivity in the Indian paper industry is declining in spite of the positive growth in labour productivity.

Table 6.3
Estimates of a Semi-log Trend

Parameter	*Estimate*	*t-ratio*
α	4.6388	202.49
β	-0.0074	-4.78

Note: Values reported in the table pertain to a semi-log equation $\ln TFP = \alpha + \beta t + \varepsilon$.

In order to look for a structural break in the level of productivity we applied sequential-Chow and CUSUM-squared tests. The results of CUSUM-squared test did not show a statistically significant structural break in TFP index while sequential Chow test[5] returned a significant F-value implying structural break during 1981-82. An implication the sequential Chow test result is that TFP might be following different growth rates for the periods comprising 1973-82 and 1982-98. In order to test for such a possibility we fitted a linear spline function to the data, the results of which indicated that difference in growth rate between the two sub-periods was not statistically significant.

Comparison with TFP from Value Added

TFP obtained from value added has been used in some of the important productivity studies on Indian industries as we observed in Chapter 5. Thus we present below results on TFP obtained by value added. It is useful to recall that there are two strands of analysis where value added is taken as a proxy for output: value added with single deflation (VASD) and value added with double deflation (VADD).

TFP obtained from value added with a single deflation procedure (TFPSD) shows an increase from 100 in 1973-74 to 106.92 in 1997-98 (see Table 6.4). Such a result is in contrast to our findings from gross output discussed earlier.

The trend growth rate estimated from a semi-log equation, however, turned out to be 0.32 per cent per annum with a t-ratio of 1.24 (see Table 6.5). Thus the positive growth rate indicated by TFPSD is not statistically significant. The R-squared also turned out to be quite low (0.06), which indicates a poor fit of the semi-log equation.

Table 6.4
TFP Index from Value Added

Year	*TFPSD*	*TFPDD*
1973-74	100.00	100.00
1974-75	83.96	88.50
1975-76	99.22	115.02
1976-77	99.76	114.42
1977-78	102.11	107.53
1978-79	101.66	103.38
1979-80	102.87	98.76
1980-81	97.55	99.23
1981-82	110.29	133.73
1982-83	83.22	69.32
1983-84	85.63	72.11
1984-85	94.11	80.36
1985-86	100.92	67.09
1986-87	98.59	72.82
1987-88	92.24	56.60
1988-89	94.88	60.95
1989-90	116.85	73.13
1990-91	118.39	81.62
1991-92	108.12	61.81
1992-93	95.09	43.71
1993-94	94.45	57.96
1994-95	88.21	66.89
1995-96	114.93	81.16
1996-97	101.09	63.56
1997-98	106.92	77.47

Note: TFPSD refers to TFP obtained from value added with single deflation while TFPDD refers to TFP from value added with double deflation.

TFP obtained from value added with double deflation (TFPDD) showed a decrease from 100 in 1973-74 to 77.47 in 1997-98 (see Table 6.4). Such a finding reinforces our earlier findings on TFP obtained from gross output. In the case of TFPDD the trend growth rate estimated from a semi-log equation is found to be -2.52 per cent per annum, with t-ratio of -4.72 (see Table 6.5). The R-squared is found to be 0.49.

When a comparison is made between the TFP growth rates obtained for the Indian paper industry through VASD and VADD, the results from VADD are found to be more appropriate than VASD for the industry. This could be because of the deflation procedure adopted in TFPDD where output and material inputs are deflated by their respective price indexes. The difference in movements of output and raw material prices, in the case of Indian paper and paper products, is quite sharp, as we would see below.

Table 6.5
TFP Growth Rates from Value Added

Method	*Growth Rate (per cent per annum)*	*t-ratio*	*R-squared*
Single Deflation	0.32	1.24	0.06
Double Deflation	-2.52	-4.72	0.49

Note: Growth rates are estimated from a semi-log equation $\ln TFP = \alpha + \beta t + \varepsilon$ by taking $\exp(\beta) - 1$. The t-ratio pertains to the estimated value $\hat{\beta}$.

It may be useful to note that there is a marked difference in the trend growth of TFPSD and TFPDD. Such a difference could be ascribed to the movement in raw material prices vis-à-vis output prices. It is worth mentioning that in the case of VASD output and intermediate inputs are deflated by the WPI of paper and paper products. On the other hand, in the case of VADD output is deflated by the WPI of paper and paper products while raw material is deflated by a price index constructed for this purpose by using the Input-Output Table.

In order to bring out the difference in price movement between raw material and output in the case of the Indian paper industry we plot the ratio of raw material price to output price[6] in Fig. 6.5. It is observed from the figure that relative raw material price witnessed a decline during the 1980s. Thus deflation of output and intermediate inputs by the same price index is likely to bring bias into TFP estimation.

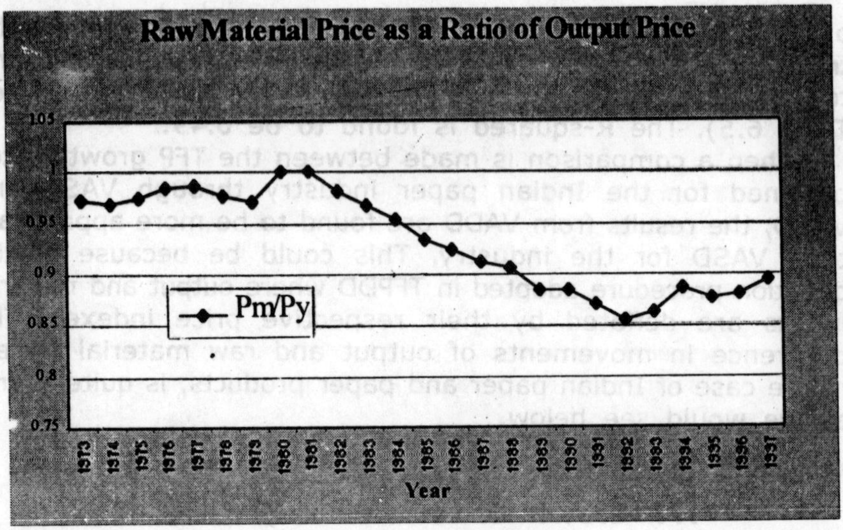

Fig. 6.5

Comparison with Earlier Results

Available estimates [Ahluwalia 1991; Banerjee 1975; Goldar 2000; Pradhan and Barik 1998, 1999a; Srivastava 2000] indicate that productivity performance of the Indian paper industry can be rated as poor as its growth rate is found to be negative in most of the studies. As can be seen from Table 6.6, estimates on growth rate in TFP for the paper industry is reported to be as low as-3.90 per cent per annum in Srivastava (2000).

Productivity estimates in the above mentioned studies are not strictly comparable due to differences in coverage, period of study and data source (see Chapter 5 for a review of these studies). Table 6.6 given below compiles TFP growth rates from selected studies on the Indian paper industry. All the studies except Banerjee (1975) have presented a translog index where the underlying production function is translog. In the case of the paper industry Banerjee (1975) estimated the growth rate in TFP by using a Solow index. Moreover, Ahluwalia (1991) used value added while Pradhan and Barik (1998, 1999a), Goldar (2000) and Srivastava (2000) used total output. However, low productivity growth in the industry is apparent from all the studies.

Another point highlighted in the studies is sub-periodic variations in the growth rate of TFP. Some of the recent studies [Goldar 2000; Srivastava 2000] on TFP have concluded that the TFP growth rate in the Indian paper industry has been higher in the 1990s compared to the 1980s. In order to have a comparative analysis on the above line we fitted a spline function with a structural break at 1990-91 to the TFP index. Such an exercise resulted in a higher TFP growth rate during the 1990s than in the 1980s, which reinforces the results of Goldar (2000) and Srivastava (2000), statistical validity of such an exercise notwithstanding. However, the difference in the TFP growth rates between the 1980s and the 1990s could not be statistically significant.

Table 6.6
TFP Estimates in Paper Industry of India

Study	*Period*	*TFPG (in per cent per annum)*
Ahluwalia (1991)	1959-60 to 1985-86	-0.7
Banerjee (1975)	1946-58	-0.003
Goldar (2000)	1981-97	-0.19
Pradhan and Barik (1998)	1963-64 to 1992-93	-0.59
Pradhan and Barik (1999a)	1963-94 to 1994-95	-0.30
Srivastava (2000)	1980-90	-3.90
	1990-96	-2.40

Notes

1. TFP growth rate in all cases is estimated through translog index except in Banerjee (1975) where it is by Solow index.
2. Estimates by Pradhan and Barik (1998, 1999a), Goldar (2000) and Srivastava (2000) are based on gross output while in other cases they are based on gross value added.
3. TFPG in Goldar (2000) and Srivastava (2000) includes printing and publishing along with paper products.
4. Srivastava (2000) used firm level data while in other cases industry level aggregate data are used.

From the above discussion we observe that the Indian paper industry has witnessed negative productivity growth during the period 1973-74 to 1997-98. The trend growth rate over this period, estimated through a semi-log equation was found to be -0.74 per cent per annum. Such a negative trend growth turned out to be statistically significant.

Analysis of partial productivity of inputs showed that labour productivity in the Indian paper industry has increased during the period of study. This is in contrast to decline in partial productivity of capital, energy and raw material. An increase in labour productivity could be because of a larger amount of capital input per worker in the industry. The capital-labour ratio has experienced an increase in the industry.

The decline in capital productivity in the industry holds much significance in view of capital scarcity in a developing economy. Decline in capital productivity implies that the efficiency of capital has decreased over time in the industry. Moreover, it indicates less than optimum utilisation of capital.

The decline in TFP level in the Indian paper industry has not been consistent and we find some variation in its level over time. In fact, the annual growth rate in TFP was found to quite erratic as a result of which the R-squared of the fitted semi-log trend could reach a level of 50 per cent only.

In order to ascertain the presence of structural breaks in the TFP growth rate over the period of study we took resort to CUSUM-squared and sequential-Chow tests. While CUSUM-squared test did not show any significant break in the trend growth rate sequential-Chow indicated the possibility of a break during the year 1981-82. Taking a clue from the Chow test, we fitted a linear spline function to TFP index with two-sub-periods separated by the year 1981-82. Results of the spline function did not show statistically significant difference in growth rates between the sub-periods.

The negative growth rate in TFP over the period 1973-98 obtained in the present study tallies with the results of existing studies on productivity growth in the industry. TFP estimates obtained from value added with single deflation did not show statistically significant change over the study period. On the other hand, TFP estimates from value added with double deflation exhibited a steeper decline than TFP obtained from gross output.

It is worth mentioning that the growth rate in TFP that we obtain by applying Divisia-Tornquist approximation involves bias because of non-fulfillment of standard assumptions underlying this method. In order to have a correct estimate of productivity growth due to pure technological change, $T\dot{F}P$ obtained in (6.5) needs to be adjusted for non-constant returns to scale, non-constant rate of capacity utilisation and price over marginal cost by appropriate coefficients obtained from econometric estimation of the translog variable cost function. Such adjustment procedure is taken up later in Chapter 8. However, in order to implement the adjustment procedure we need to have estimates on production characteristics of the industry such as capacity utilisation, scale economies and mark-up. These characteristics are derived from the parameter estimates of a cost function. Keeping in view our basic premise that production technology in the Indian paper industry is characterised by a translog variable cost function, we describe its estimation procedure below.

Notes

1. The dual to an arbitrary production function (6.1) considered is given by $C = C(P, Y, t)$ where *P* is a vector of input prices, *Y* is level of output and *t* is the time variable indicating technological progress.
2. In Chapter 5 we had mentioned that $T\dot{F}P$ can be estimated from the dual cost function also. This is possible by subtracting the growth rate in average cost from the weighted factor prices growth rate. See Chambers (1988).
3. Here a kinked curve is fitted to the data so that the growth rate may differ across segments but remain uniform within a sub-period. The advantage of using a spline function is that there is no discontinuity between the segments of the kinked line. However, there are discontinuities in the time derivative of a spline function.
4. It may be recalled that the present analysis is based on 4 per cent per annum depreciation in capital input. When no depreciation in capital stock is allowed, the TFP index declined from 100 in 1973-74 to 89.06 in 1997-98.
5. The sequential Chow test divides the sample into two sub-samples at every possible point for estimating differences in growth rates. The difference between the sub-periods is tested on the basis of a significant F-value.
6. This point has been emphasised in Balakrishnan and Pushpangadan (1994) in the case of the Indian aggregate manufacturing industries.

7

Contribution of TFP to Output Growth

In the preceding chapter, we examined the nature TFP growth witnessed in the Indian paper industry. It was found, on the basis of Divisia-Tornquist approximation, that the industry registered negative TFP growth at the rate of -0.57 per cent per annum during the period 1973-74 to 1997-98. Such a result was obtained by subtracting the revenue share weighted input growth rate from the output growth rate. Thus a negative TFP growth rate has the implication that the input growth rate was higher in the industry than the output growth rate. It is, therefore, pertinent to examine the sources of output growth in the industry. Particularly, the contribution of TFP to output growth is the major issue pursued in this chapter.

Decomposition Studies in India

Researchers have decomposed the output growth rate according to its originating sources, which can be ascribed to either the utilisation of factor inputs or the contribution of TFP [see, for example, Ahluwalia 1985, Goldar 1986 and Srivastava 1996 for decomposition analysis in the Indian context]. These studies come out with an inference that the contribution of TFP to output growth in Indian manufacturing industries is either low or negative. In the case of the Indian paper industry Ahluwalia (1985) found that TFP contributed 13.58 per cent to output (value added) growth during the period 1959-80. In contrast to this Pradhan and Barik (1999a) found a negative TFP contribution of -4.47 per cent to output growth for the period 1963-64 to 1994-95. The result of Pradhan and Barik is supported by Srivastava (1996) who found a negative TFP contribution to the extent of -66.07 per cent during 1980-90 in the case of public limited companies in the Indian paper industry.

Decomposition studies on Indian industries have followed two distinct approaches to measurement of TFP and factor contributions. While Ahluwalia (1985) and Srivastava (1996) undertook decomposition analysis with the help of growth accounting or an index number approach, Pradhan and Barik (1999a) estimated factor and TFP contributions through econometric estimation of a translog production function in line with Boskin and Lau (1990).

While the essence of decomposition studies is to identify the contribution of TFP to output growth, Krugman (1994) postulates, on the basis of growth performance in East Asian countries, that the extent of contribution made by TFP determines the long-run sustainability of an economy. Particularly, if a high growth rate results from factor accumulation without TFP growth, long-run sustainability of such growth is doubtful. Application of Krugman's thesis to the Indian paper industry would enable us to ascertain the nature of growth in the industry.

Method of Analysis

In the present study we estimate the contribution of TFP to output growth econometrically with the help of a translog production function. For this purpose we first estimate a translog production function for the Indian paper industry. As mentioned in Chapter 3 we use industry level annual data taken from ASI for the period 1973-74 to 1997-98. Secondly, we estimate the marginal contribution of TFP to output from the parameter estimates of the translog production function. We outline the estimation procedure for attaining these objectives below.

Estimation of a Translog Production Function

In our attempt to identify the contribution of TFP to output growth we use a translog production function with four inputs (*K*, *L*, *E*, *M*). The regression equation selected for this purpose takes the form:

$$\ln Y = \beta_0 + \sum_i \beta_i \ln X_i + \frac{1}{2}\sum_i\sum_j \beta_{ij} \ln X_i \ln X_j$$

$$+ \beta_t t + \sum_i \beta_{it}\, t \ln X_i + \frac{1}{2}\beta_{tt} t^2 + \varepsilon \qquad (i, j = K, L, E, M) \qquad ...(7.1)$$

where Y = output

X_i = i^{th} input

t = time variable

ε = error term.

The procedure adopted for estimating (7.1) assumes the production function to be homogeneous of degree one, i.e., it yields constant returns to scale. Therefore, its parameters are adjusted to satisfy the following conditions.

$$\sum_i \alpha_i = 1, \ \sum_i \beta_{ij} = 0, \ \sum_i \beta_{it} = 0 \quad \text{and } \beta_{ij} = \beta_{ji} \qquad ...(7.2)$$

$(i, j = K, L, E, M)$

On differentiating (7.1) with respect to inputs (X_i) and applying the producers' equilibrium condition, $\frac{\partial Y}{\partial X_i} = \frac{P_i}{P_Y}$ (P_i = price of X_i and P_Y = price of Y), the ith share equation obtained is

$$s_i = \beta_i + \sum_j \beta_{ij}\, ln\ X_j + \beta_{it} t \qquad ...(7.3)$$

$(i, j = K, L, E, M)$

We estimate the production function (7.1) together with

the revenue share equations (7.3) by Zellner's method so that the information contained in the input demand functions are taken into account. As the sum of the four factor shares, *K, L, E* and *M,* is unity, the problem of linear dependency and consequent singularity of the residual covariance matrix is avoided by dropping one of the share equations. The present study drops the material inputs share equation[1]. Restrictions in (7.2) are imposed to the system of equations to satisfy the linear homogeneity condition on the production function.

Estimation of TFP and Factor Contributions

The study derives the factor and TFP contributions from an estimated translog production function in which the average growth rate in output over the period of analysis is given by

$$\dot{Y} = \frac{1}{T}[\ln \hat{Y}(K_T, L_T, E_T, M_T, T) - \ln \hat{Y}(K_0, L_0, E_0, M_0, 0)] \qquad ...(7.4)$$

where $\dot{Y}$ = growth rate in output,

T = time variable for the final period

0 = time variable for the initial period

$\hat{Y}$ = estimated value of output as obtained from (7.1), and subscripts T and 0 are used for indicating the level of inputs at final and initial periods respectively.

The growth rate of output obtained from (7.4) is decomposed into the contributions of inputs X_i (i = *K, L, E, M*) and TFP. In such a formulation the contribution of X_i is defined as the increase in output solely due to increase *in* X_i, when the level of other inputs and technology (time) remain unchanged [Boskin and Lau 1990, *cited in* Felipe 1997]. For example, the contribution of *K* at the initial time period *0*, denoted by C_{K0}, is given by

$$C_{K0} = \frac{1}{T}[\ln \hat{Y}(K_T, L_0, E_0, M_0, 0) - \ln \hat{Y}(K_0, L_0, E_0, M_0, 0)] \qquad ...(7.5)$$

It may be noted that the contribution of *K* will change over time unless technical change is Hicks-neutral. In the presence of technical bias the contribution of *K* at the final time period *T* is

$$C_{KT} = \frac{1}{T}[\ln \hat{Y}(K_T, L_T, E_T, M_T, T) - \ln \hat{Y}(K_0, L_T, E_T, M_T, T)] \quad ...(7.6)$$

The average contribution of *K* over the study period is obtained as

$$\dot{C}_K = \frac{1}{2}(C_{K0} + C_{KT}) \quad ...(7.7)$$

For deriving the contribution of TFP at the initial time period *0*, $C_{TFP,0}$, to the growth rate in output, $\dot{Y}$, the equation used is

$$C_{TFP,0} = \frac{1}{T}[\ln \hat{Y}(K_0, L_0, E_0, M_0, T) - \ln \hat{Y}(K_0, L_0, E_0, M_0, 0)] \quad ...(7.8)$$

Similarly, its contribution at time *T* is given by

$$C_{TFP,T} = \frac{1}{T}[\ln \hat{Y}(K_T, L_T, E_T, M_T, T) - \ln \hat{Y}(K_T, L_T, E_T, M_T, 0)] \quad ...(7.9)$$

The average contribution of TFPG over the period of study is computed as

$$C_{TFP} = \frac{1}{2}(C_{TFP,T} + C_{TFP,0}) \quad ...(7.10)$$

Decomposition Through Growth Accounting Approach

In the growth accounting approach, decomposition of output growth into contributions of inputs and TFP is derived by taking logarithmic derivative of a production function. For an arbitrary production function, $Y = f(X,t)$, it is given by

$$\frac{d \ln Y}{dt} = \sum_i \frac{\partial \ln f}{\partial \ln X_i} \frac{\partial \ln X_i}{\partial t} + \frac{\partial \ln f}{\partial t}$$

On application of the first order condition of producer equilibrium ($\frac{\partial f}{\partial X_i} = \frac{P_i}{P_Y}$) to the above we obtain

$$\frac{d\ln Y}{dt} = \sum_i \frac{P_i X_i}{P_Y Y} \frac{\partial \ln X_i}{\partial t} + \frac{\partial \ln f}{\partial t}$$

In symbols,

$$\dot{Y} = \sum_i s_i \dot{X}_i + \dot{TFP} \qquad ...(7.11)$$

where $s_i = \frac{P_i X_i}{P_Y Y}$ is the expenditure share of ith input in revenue, and dot over a variable indicates the growth rate in it.

In (7.11) $s_i \dot{X}_i$ indicates the contribution of the ith input to the output growth rate $\dot{Y}$ while $\dot{TFP}$ indicates the contribution of TFP.

Empirical Findings

As the contribution of TFP is derived from the translog production function, first we note the features of the estimated translog production function (7.1). Secondly, we discuss the results on the contribution of TFP and factor inputs to the output growth rate along with their implications. Finally, we present the results obtained from application of the growth accounting method for a comparative analysis.

Estimates of Translog Production Function

Using industry level annual data of the Indian paper industry for the period 1973-74 to 1997-98 we estimated a translog production function, the coefficients of which are reported in Table 7.1. It is seen from the table that 13 out of 21 coefficients are statistically significant at the 5 per cent level. The production function seems to have a good fit, as the R-squared between actual and predicted values of ln*Y* is found to be 98.7%.

The estimated production function satisfies the regularity conditions of monotonicity and concavity at all the observations. The monotonicity condition is met, as estimated factor shares are positive at every sample point. The concavity condition, which has been seen through the negative semi-definiteness of the Hessian matrix, is fulfilled by the estimated coefficients at all the observations.

Table 7.1
Estimates of Translog Production Function in Indian Paper Industry: 1973-98

Parameter	*Estimate*	*t-ratio*
β_0	11.2680	380.48*
β_K	0.2708	18.09*
β_L	0.1191	36.63*
β_E	0.1086	15.11*
β_M	0.5015	54.47*
β_{KK}	0.0694	1.16
β_{LL}	0.0482	4.00*
β_{EE}	0.0731	2.65*
β_{MM}	0.1351	4.66*
β_{KL}	-0.0208	-1.70
β_{KE}	0.0303	0.94
β_{KM}	-0.0789	-2.49*
β_{LE}	-0.0373	-3.27*
β_{LM}	0.0099	0.81
β_{EM}	-0.0661	-2.63*
β_t	-0.0090	-1.91
β_{tt}	0.0001	0.43
β_{Kt}	-0.0033	-2.91*
β_{Lt}	-0.0001	-0.14
β_{Et}	0.0003	0.35
β_{Mt}	0.0031	3.76*

Notes: The estimated coefficients given in the table pertain to translog production function (7.1) given in the text.
*indicates statistical significance at the 5 per cent level.

Estimates of TFP and Factor Contribution

The results of the decomposition analysis are presented in Table 7.2. It is seen from the table that TFP has a negative contribution of -1.15 per cent to output growth during the period 1973-74 to 1997-98. That has the implication that TFP worked as a drag on output growth. Secondly, the contribution of inputs outweighs the output growth rate. It is observed from the table that the contribution of inputs, taken together, is 101.15 per cent of output growth. That shows a relatively higher rate of growth in inputs than in output. This implies an increase in inefficiency in resource utilisation over time. Thirdly, the findings on the contribution of TFP to output growth reinforces our earlier finding (in Chapter 6) that the trend growth rate in TFP in the Indian paper industry has been negative at a rate of -0.74 per cent per annum during the period 1973-74 to 1997-98.

Table 7.2
Factor and TFP Contribution to Output Growth: Econometric Method
(1973-74 to 1997-98)

Factor	*Contribution in per cent*
Capital (K)	29.56
Labour (L)	5.45
Energy (E)	12.37
Material (M)	53.77
TFP	-1.15

Note: Contributions of factors and TFP are obtained econometrically as per discussion in the text.

After ascertaining the contribution of TFP to output growth a discussion on the individual contributions of factor inputs is in order. It is found from the table that non-energy raw material (*M*) contributed the maximum at 53.77 per cent to output growth. On the other hand, the findings showed that labour contributed the minimum at 5.45 per cent of output growth. Of the remaining two inputs, capital contributed 29.56 per cent while energy contributed 12.37 per cent of output growth.

The low contribution of labour input to output growth in the Indian paper industry needs to be examined together with the finding of increasing labour productivity as reported in the previous chapter (see Table 6.1). It is useful to point out that the contribution of labour is given by the product of the labour share in revenue and the growth rate in labour input ($S_L \cdot \dot{L}$). In the case of the Indian paper industry while labour has increased at a rate of 2.52 per cent per annum during 1973-74 to 1997-98, the wage share in revenue has decreased from 17.1 per cent in 1973-74 to 9.3 per cent in 1997-98. Consequently the contribution of labour turns out to be low. On the other hand, improvement in labour productivity can be attributed to an increase in amount of capital per labour in the industry. As observed in Chapter 6, the capital-labour ratio (normalised for the beginning year) in the Indian paper industry has increased from 100 in 1973-74 to 255.68 in 1997-98. Thus labour input is accompanied by an increasing amount of capital, which in turn is improving its efficiency.

The findings of the decomposition analysis have important policy implications for the Indian paper industry. Output growth in the industry has come through neither technological progress nor capital accumulation. Rather it is propelled by utilisation of intermediate inputs, i.e., energy and raw material. It is observed from Table 7.2 that 69.14 per cent of output growth in the industry is contributed by intermediate inputs.

The finding that growth in the Indian paper industry is intermediate input-driven raises the issue of long-run sustainability of the industry. Depleting forest-reserves and consequent shortages of raw material have been a prominent feature of the industry. In order to alleviate the problem of material input shortage the government has taken certain policy initiatives such as encouragement of unconventional resource based plants. However, the effectiveness of such policy is questionable, as the industry has resorted to import of paper grade pulp, waste paper as well as paper product, which is increasing over time [Government of India (c)].

A second issue that deserves attention is the pollution load of the industry. It is observed in a study by Hartman *et al.* (1997) that a material intensive production process is pollution intensive in the case of the paper industry in Asian countries. In fact, the paper industry in India is categorised as one of the seventeen most polluting industries [Government of India 1997]. In order to reduce the polluting behaviour of the industry, its material intensity needs to be checked through appropriate technological developments.

Results from Growth Accounting Method

The results of the growth accounting method on decomposition analysis reinforce our findings from the econometric method. The results of the growth accounting method are presented in Table 7.3. It is seen from the table that TFP contributed negatively to output growth at -5.8 per cent of output growth. This is in line with our earlier finding from econometric approach.

Among the inputs considered in the study, non-energy raw

material (*M*) contributed the maximum at 56.58 per cent to output growth (see Table 7.3) while labour contributed the lowest at 4.33 per cent. Capital had a contribution of 28.57 per cent while energy contributed 16.31 per cent. The relative contributions of inputs are similar to those obtained in the econometric approach.

Table 7.3
Factor and TFP Contributions to Output Growth: Growth Accounting Method

	Contribution of (in per cent)				
Period	*K*	*L*	*E*	*M*	*TFP*
1973-98	28.57	4.33	16.31	56.58	-5.80
1973-80	28.07	8.91	16.28	45.53	1.21
1980-90	25.17	1.58	22.12	63.51	-12.38
1990-98	33.97	4.63	7.81	55.43	-1.84

Note: Figures in the table refer to average contribution over the study period.

We stretched the decomposition analysis into a sub-period analysis across decades, the results of which are presented in Table 7.3. The results of sub-period analysis did not alter the conclusion that output growth in the Indian paper industry is contributed mostly by factor inputs. It is observed from Table 7.3 that the combined contribution of inputs varied between 98.79 per cent during 1973-80 and 112.38 per cent during 1980-90. Secondly, the feature of negative contribution by TFP remains valid in the decomposition analysis across decades, except in 1973-80, during which it made a positive contribution of 1.21 per cent. Thirdly, the 1980s turned out to be the most inefficient period from a resource-utilisation point of view as TFP contributed -12.38 per cent to output growth. However, during the period 1990-98 the negative contribution of TFP dropped to -1.84 per cent of output growth.

In the sub-period analysis material input made the largest contribution to output growth in all the sub-periods although its contribution varied between 45.53 per cent during 1973-80 and 63.51 per cent during 1980-90. Thus the inference on long-run sustainability and polluting behaviour remains valid in the sub-period analysis also.

There are minor differences in the estimates obtained from econometric and growth accounting approaches for factor and TFP contributions. Such differences could be ascribed to *(i)* biased technical change that was captured through the econometric estimation; *(ii)* the econometric method giving an average growth rate between the last and first observations while the growth accounting method indicates the trend growth.

The negative contribution of TFP to output growth has serious policy implications. The raw material driven growth process found in the Indian paper industry raises the issues of long-run sustainability of the industry and its environment-friendly behaviour. In the event of depleting forest reserves and consequent shortage of locally available resources, the industry is increasingly resorting to imports of intermediate inputs such as paper grade pulp and waste paper. Nonetheless, inefficiency in utilisation of resources was found to be a distinct feature of the study.

Note

1. Similar to the estimation of the translog cost function we drop the material inputs share equation, although the estimates are invariant to the share equation dropped [Christensen and Greene 1976].

8

Isolation of Technological Progress

The concept of TFP, postulated as a residual, crucially depends upon fulfilment of certain restrictive assumptions such as constant returns to scale, full utilisation of capacity and presence of perfect competition in the product market. In cases when these conditions are not met, TFP includes the effects of scale economies, capacity utilisation and mark-up over marginal cost. Nonetheless, the effects of these factors can be purged from TFP and for this purpose we require appropriate estimates of various characteristics that describe production structure of the industry.

The Indian paper industry, as we observed in Chapter 4, exploited the advantage of scale economies, although under-utilisation of capacity, imperfect market conditions and a mark-up over marginal cost were its distinct features. Presence of such features in the production structure of the industry would make the Solow residual a biased estimate of technological progress. Thus our estimates of the growth rate in TFP obtained through Divisia-Tornquist approximation and presented in Chapter 6 provide only a poor representation of technological change in the industry.

The effect of scale economies, capacity utilisation and mark-up on TFP are distinct. It is useful to recall that the Solow residual is obtained by subtracting the revenue share weighted input growth rate from the output growth rate. In the presence of scale economies cost is less than revenue so that cost share would exceed revenue share. Thus real productivity growth would be less than the observed Solow residual based on revenue share, thereby making TFP an overestimate of productivity growth. Similarly, in the case of chronic excess capacity the industry's observed costs would be more than the optimum at full capacity utilisation. As a result, the appropriate cost share would be less than revenue share and TFP would be an under-estimate of productivity growth. On the other hand, in the presence of mark-up, the price-marginal cost ratio would exceed unity and a higher value would be assigned to the input growth rate than warranted. Thus TFP would be an under-estimate of productivity growth. The combined effects of all three factors, however, cannot be ascertained beforehand as the effects are in opposite directions.

The adjustment in TFP to purge the effects of factors such as economies of scale, under-utilisation of capacity and mark-up can be divided into two broad categories. While scale economies and capacity utilisation require supply side adjustments, purging the effects of mark-up is approached from the demand side. Keeping this in view we present theoretical background to the adjustment procedure in the next two sections. Finally, empirical estimates of technological change in the Indian paper industry are given.

Adjustment for Scale Economies and Capacity Utilisation

In order to purge the effects of scale economies and CU we proceed as follows: First, we establish a relationship, attributed largely to Ohta (1974), between technological progress and TFP in a full static equilibrium (FSE) framework. Second, the partial static equilibrium considerations are introduced and the relationship between scale economies and capacity utilisation is examined on the lines of Morrison (1988a). Consequently, as will be seen below, adjustment of TFP for short-run scale economies would be attempted to purge the effects of both long-run scale economies and CU.

It is useful to recall from Chapter 5 that theoretically we obtain an identical TFP value whether it is estimated from the production function $Y = f(X,t)$ or the cost function $C = C(P,Y,t)$ because of the duality properties of technology. Thus we have TFP measures from the primal formulation $\varepsilon_{Yt} = \frac{\partial \ln f}{\partial t}$ and from the dual, $\varepsilon_{Ct} = \frac{\partial \ln C}{\partial t}$, which are equivalent under standard assumptions such as constant returns to scale (CRTS), full utilisation of capacity and perfect competition in the product market [Chambers 1988].

Adjustment for Scale Economies

Adjustment of TFP for non-fulfilment of CRTS requires certain modification in the Solow residual. However, before effecting such a modification we establish a relationship between ε_{Yt} and ε_{Ct} in a long-run equilibrium framework. This is worth consideration as the linking factor between these two is scale economies[1].

In order to derive estimates for the primal TFP measure ε_{Yt} we take the logarithmic total derivative of the production function $Y = f(X,t)$ such that

$$\frac{d\ln Y}{dt} = \sum_i \frac{\partial f}{\partial X_i}\frac{X_i}{Y}\frac{\partial \ln X_i}{\partial t} + \frac{\partial \ln f}{\partial t} \qquad ...(8.1)$$

From the first order condition of producer equilibrium we know that $\frac{\partial f}{\partial X_i} = \frac{P_i}{P_Y}$ under CRTS and perfect competition. Thus

$$\frac{d\ln Y}{dt} = \sum_i \frac{P_i X_i}{P_Y Y}\frac{\partial \ln X_i}{\partial t} + \frac{\partial \ln f}{\partial t}$$

which is given by

$$\varepsilon_{Yt} = \dot{Y} - \sum_i s_i \dot{X}_i \qquad ...(8.2)$$

It is useful to note that (8.2) is the same as the Solow residual given in Chapter 6. However, in the absence of CRTS, $\frac{\partial f}{\partial X_i} \neq \frac{P_i}{P_Y}$ and the producer equilibrium condition is given by

$\frac{\partial f}{\partial X_i} = \frac{P_i}{\partial C/\partial Y}$ where $\frac{\partial C}{\partial Y}$ is marginal cost[2]. By substituting this in (8.1) we get

$$\varepsilon_{Yt} = \dot{Y} - \sum_i \frac{P_i}{\partial C/\partial Y}\frac{X_i}{Y}\dot{X}_i$$

$$\text{or,}\quad \varepsilon_{Yt} = \dot{Y} - \sum_i \frac{P_i X_i}{C} \frac{C/Y}{\partial C/\partial Y} \dot{X}_i$$

$$\text{or,}\quad \varepsilon_{Yt} = \dot{Y} - \frac{1}{\varepsilon_{CY}} \sum_i \frac{P_i X_i}{C} \dot{X}_i \qquad \text{...(8.3)}$$

On the other hand, from the dual side ε_{Ct} is estimated by taking the logarithmic total derivative of the cost function $C = C(P, Y, t)$ with respect to t. Thus

$$\frac{d \ln C}{dt} = \sum_i \frac{\partial \ln C}{\partial \ln P_i} \frac{\partial \ln P_i}{\partial t} + \frac{\partial \ln C}{\partial \ln Y} \frac{\partial \ln Y}{\partial t} + \frac{\partial \ln C}{\partial t} \qquad \text{...(8.4)}$$

$$\text{or,}\quad \dot{C} = \sum_i \frac{\partial C}{\partial P_i} \frac{P_i}{C} \dot{P}_i + \varepsilon_{CY} \dot{Y} + \varepsilon_{Ct}$$

Rearranging terms in (8.4) and applying Shephard's lemma, that is, $\frac{\partial C}{\partial P_i} = X_i$ it is shown that

$$\varepsilon_{Ct} = \dot{C} - \sum_i \frac{P_i X_i}{C} \dot{P}_i - \varepsilon_{CY} \dot{Y} \qquad \text{...(8.5)}$$

However, total cost is the sum of expenditure on all inputs, that is, $C = \sum_i P_i X_i$. Totally differentiating it with respect to *t* we get

$$\frac{dC}{dt} = \sum_i \left(P_i \frac{\partial X_i}{\partial t} + X_i \frac{\partial P_i}{\partial t}\right)$$

$$\text{or,}\quad \frac{1}{C}\frac{dC}{dt} = \sum_i \left(\frac{P_i X_i}{C} \frac{\partial X_i}{\partial t} \frac{1}{X_i} + \frac{P_i X_i}{C} \frac{\partial P_i}{\partial t} \frac{1}{P_i}\right)$$

$$\text{or,}\quad \dot{C} = \sum_i \frac{P_i X_i}{C} \dot{X}_i + \sum_i \frac{P_i X_i}{C} \dot{P}_i$$

$$\text{or,}\quad \dot{C} - \sum_i \frac{P_i X_i}{C} \dot{P}_i = \sum_i \frac{P_i X_i}{C} \dot{X}_i \qquad \text{...(8.6)}$$

By substituting (8.6) in (8.5) we get

$$\varepsilon_{Ct} = \sum_i \frac{P_i X_i}{C} \dot{X}_i - \varepsilon_{CY} \dot{Y}$$

which can be modified to

$$-\varepsilon_{Ct} = \varepsilon_{CY} \dot{Y} - \sum_i \frac{P_i X_i}{C} \dot{X}_i \qquad \text{...(8.7)}$$

By comparing (8.3) and (8.7) we draw two major inferences. First, when there is CRTS, $\varepsilon_{CY} = 1$ and $C = P_Y Y$, the TFP estimate from the primal formulation is equivalent to the negative of its dual estimate such that $\varepsilon_{Yt} = -\varepsilon_{Ct}$. Thus both primal and dual measures are equivalent to the growth rate in TFP in the case of CRTS, that is, $\varepsilon_{Yt} = -\varepsilon_{Ct} = \dot{TFP}$. Second, when scale economies are present, the primal TFP measure (ε_{Yt}) is the product of the negative of the dual TFP measure ($-\varepsilon_{Ct}$) and the degree of returns to scale (ε_{CY}^{-1}), such that

$$\varepsilon_{Yt} = -\varepsilon_{Ct}\varepsilon_{CY}^{-1} \qquad \text{...(8.8)}$$

An implication of (8.8) is that in the presence of economies of scale TFP is an over-estimate of technological progress and an under-estimate in case of diseconomies of scale. In either case, TFP adjusted for non-CRTS is given by (8.7).

Adjustment for CU

A major limitation of the adjustment procedure in (8.7) is that it is based on a long-run equilibrium framework. In the case of short-run fixity of capital input, there is the possibility that production capacity is not utilised fully. Moreover, the industry is in a position to change the level of output by changing the levels of variable inputs, not the level of quasi-fixed capital, which is brought to its equilibrium level only in the long-run. Thus there is a distinction between short-run and long-run scale economies (see Chapter 2) which are linked by the rate of capacity utilisation.

In the production process, a change in total cost due to variation in output is given by two parts: response to variable inputs keeping capital as fixed and response to variations in capital. Thus

$$\frac{d\ln C}{d\ln Y}=\frac{dC}{dY}\cdot\frac{Y}{C}=\frac{Y}{C}\left(\left.\frac{\partial C}{\partial Y}\right|_{K=\bar{K}}+\frac{\partial C}{\partial K}\cdot\frac{dK}{dY}\right) \quad \text{...(8.9)}$$

Using the notation followed in the study, (8.9) is given by

$$\eta=\varepsilon_{CY}+\frac{\partial C}{\partial K}\cdot\frac{K}{C}\cdot\frac{dK}{dY}\cdot\frac{Y}{K}=\varepsilon_{CY}+\varepsilon_{CK}\cdot\eta_K$$

where $\eta_K=\dfrac{d\ln K}{d\ln Y}$ is the inverse of returns to capital input. The above can be rearranged as

$$\varepsilon_{CY}=\eta-\varepsilon_{CK}\cdot\eta_K=\eta(1-\frac{\eta_K}{\eta}\varepsilon_{CK}) \quad \text{...(8.10)}$$

In (8.10) we observe that ε_{CY} is the cost flexibility in the short-run while η is cost flexibility in the long-run. Thus we have the relationship

$$\varepsilon_{CY}^{SR}=CU\cdot\varepsilon_{CY}^{LR} \quad \text{...(8.11)}$$

where $\varepsilon_{CY}^{LR}=\eta$, and *CU* is given by $(1-\dfrac{\eta_K}{\eta}\varepsilon_{CK})$.

Estimating Equation in the Presence of Scale Economies and CU

The relationship portrayed in (8.11) is used to eliminate the effects of CU and (long-run) scale economies from TFP. In (8.7) we replace ε_{CY} by $CU\cdot\eta$ and find productivity growth adjusted for scale economies and capacity utilisation as follows:

$$-\dot{\varepsilon}_{Ct}=\eta\,.\,CU\,.\,\dot{Y}-\sum_i\frac{PX_i}{C}\dot{X}_i \quad \text{...(8.12)}$$

By using estimates of and CU presented in Chapter 4 for the Indian paper industry in (8.12) we are in a position to obtain scale economies and CU adjusted TFP for the industry.

Adjustment for Mark-up

The adjustment for market power is somewhat different from that of scale economies and capacity utilisation in the sense that it is a demand side adjustment in contrast to that of supply side, while considering scale economies and CU [Morrison 1992]. Let us start with the logarithmic derivative of the production function such that

$$\frac{d\ln Y}{dt} = \sum_i \frac{\partial f}{\partial X_i}\frac{X_i}{Y}\frac{\partial \ln X_i}{\partial t} + \frac{\partial \ln f}{\partial t} \quad \text{...(8.13)}$$

In general, the producer equilibrium condition is given by $\frac{\partial f}{\partial X_i} = \frac{P_i}{\partial C/\partial Y}$ where $\frac{\partial C}{\partial Y}$ is marginal cost. By substituting this in (8.13) we get

$$\varepsilon_{Yt} = \dot{Y} - \sum_i \frac{P_i}{\partial C/\partial Y}\frac{X_i}{Y}\dot{X}_i$$

$$\text{or,} \quad \varepsilon_{Yt} = \dot{Y} - \sum_i \frac{P_Y}{MC}\frac{P_i X_i}{P_Y Y}\dot{X}_i$$

$$\text{or,} \quad \varepsilon_{Yt} = \dot{Y} - \frac{P_Y}{MC}\sum_i \frac{P_i X_i}{P_Y Y}\dot{X}_i \quad \text{...(8.14)}$$

Since

$$\frac{P}{MC} = \frac{P}{P + Y\cdot\partial P/\partial Y} = \frac{P}{P(1 + Y/P\cdot\partial P/\partial Y)} = \frac{P}{P(1+\partial\ln P/\partial \ln Y)} \quad \text{...(8.15)}$$

We know from the inverse output demand equation (2.36) (see Chapter 2) that $\frac{\partial \ln P}{\partial \ln Y} = \alpha_Y$. By substituting this in (8.15) we find that

$$\varepsilon_{Y_t}^{M} = \dot{Y} - \frac{1}{1+\alpha_Y}\sum_i \frac{P_i X_i}{P_Y Y}\dot{X}_i \qquad \text{...(8.16)}$$

where $\varepsilon_{Y_t}^{M}$ is mark-up-adjusted TFP growth.

We observe that (8.16) provides a correct estimate of productivity when the effect of mark-up is present.

Adjustment for CU, Scale Economies and Mark-up

In the presence of all three features, viz., scale economies, capacity utilisation and mark-up we have to adjust for all three factors so as to isolate technological progress. For this purpose we make use of the equations (8.8) and (8.16).

It has been shown by Park and Kwon (1995) that the basic relationship of $\varepsilon_{Y_t} = -\varepsilon_{C_t}\varepsilon_{CY}^{-1}$ holds good in the case of partial static equilibrium also. On application of this relation to (8.16) we have

$$-\varepsilon_{C_t}^{A} = \varepsilon_{CY}\left[\dot{Y} - \frac{1}{1+\alpha_Y}\sum_i \frac{P_i X_i}{P_Y Y}\dot{X}_i\right] \qquad \text{...(8.17)}$$

where $-\varepsilon_{C_t}^{A}$ represents TFP adjusted all three factors, viz., scale economies, CU and mark-up.

As the effects of all three factors are removed from TFP, (8.17) presents a more precise estimate of productivity growth representing technological change in an industry. We provide below the empirical results on application of the above adjustment methods to the Indian paper industry.

Empirical Findings

Based on the adjustment procedure discussed above we purged the effects of scale economies, CU and mark-up from traditional TFP of the Indian paper industry, which provided us with an estimate of technological progress (TP). In this exercise we made use of the TFP estimates presented in Chapter 6 and estimates of scale economies, CU and mark-up presented in Chapter 4.

Bias in Traditional TFP Measure

The results on adjusted TFP growth rates are given in Table 8.1 along with the traditional TFP growth rates. It is seen from the table that TFP is an underestimate of TP in the Indian paper industry during the period 1973-74 to 1997-98. The annual average growth rate in traditional TFP was found to be -0.33 per cent. On the other hand, the annual average growth rate in TP was found to be 5.59 per cent. Thus traditional TFP exhibits a downward bias of -5.92 per cent per annum, on average. The downward bias present in traditional TFP has been reported in studies on industrial productivity outside India [see, for example, Morrison 1992 and Park and Kwon 1995, among others].

A close relationship is found between growth rates of TFP and TP. The correlation coefficient between the growth rates in TFP and TP was found to be 0.74. However, the growth rate of TFP turned out to be below that of TP for all the years, except four, during the period of study (see Fig. 8.1).

Trend Growth in TP

We constructed an index of productivity on the basis of annual growth rates in TP (see Table 8.2), similar to the TFP index constructed in Chapter 6. Such an index was found to have increased from 100 in 1973-74 to 414.35 in 1997-98. A consistent increase in the index, except for minor decline in a few years, was observed in the TP index (see Fig. 8.2, which plots the TP index against time).

In order to ascertain a trend growth rate in the estimated TP index, we fitted a semi-log equation to it. Such an exercise showed that the Indian paper industry witnessed a trend growth rate of 6.54 per cent per annum. The trend growth rate was found to be statistically significant at the 1 per cent level as the t-ratio was 29.22. Moreover, the semi-log equation was found to have a good fit as R-squared turned out to be 97.3 per cent.

Diverse Trends in TFP and TP

An important finding of the study is concerning the negative growth in TFP in spite of substantial technological progress. Such discrepancy in TFP is ascribed to the decline in degree of returns to scale and rate of capacity utilisation. It is useful to recall that degree of returns to scale in the Indian paper industry declined from 1.55 in 1974-75 to 1.32 in 1997-98. Similarly, rate of capacity utilisation declined from 81.86 per cent in 1973-74 to 76.94 per cent in 1997-98.

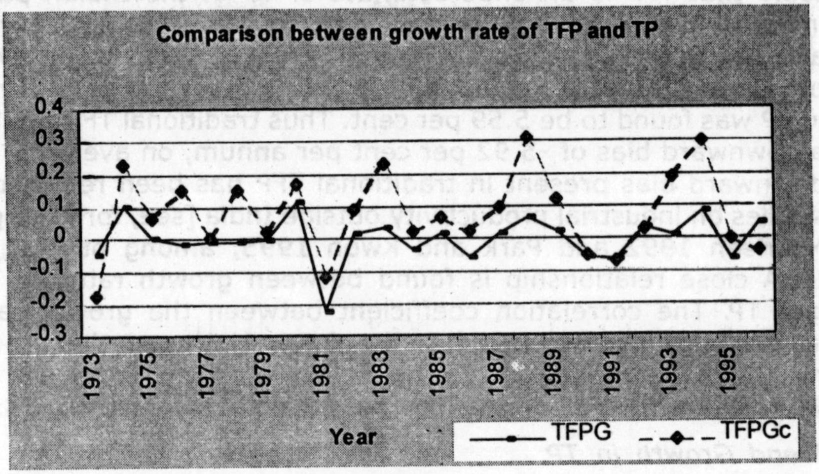

Fig. 8.1

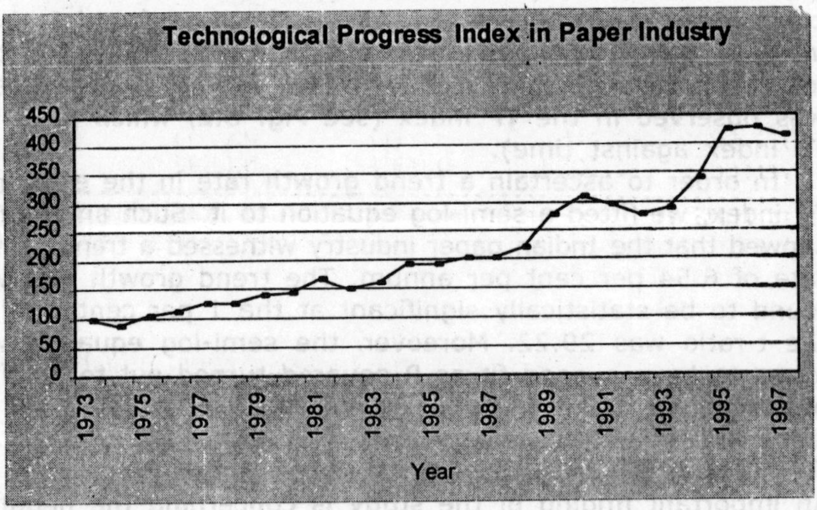

Fig. 8.2

Table 8.1
Extent of Bias in Traditional TFP

Year	*TFPG*	$-\varepsilon_{Ct}^{A}$	*Bias in TFP*
1973-74	0.0006	-0.0244	0.0251
1974-75	-0.0501	-0.1174	0.0672
1975-76	0.1020	0.1866	-0.0846
1976-77	-0.0017	0.0497	-0.0514
1977-78	-0.0194	0.1109	-0.1302
1978-79	-0.0145	-0.0026	-0.0119
1979-80	-0.0121	0.1111	-0.1232
1980-81	-0.0028	0.0281	-0.0308
1981-82	0.1118	0.1508	-0.0390
1982-83	-0.2257	-0.1141	-0.1116
1983-84	0.0104	0.0697	-0.0593
1984-85	0.0324	0.1837	-0.1513
1985-86	-0.0361	-0.0047	-0.0314
1986-87	0.0136	0.0559	-0.0423
1987-88	-0.0575	0.0097	-0.0672
1988-89	0.0128	0.0742	-0.0615
1989-90	0.0622	0.2353	-0.1731
1990-91	0.0186	0.1011	-0.0825
1991-92	-0.0604	-0.0458	-0.0146
1992-93	-0.0687	-0.0560	-0.0127
1993-94	0.0344	0.0313	0.0031
1994-95	0.0079	0.1657	-0.1578
1995-96	0.0792	0.2282	-0.1489
1996-97	-0.0640	0.0014	-0.0653
1997-98	0.0451	-0.0312	0.0763
Average	-0.0033	0.0559	-0.0592

Notes: TFPG and $-\varepsilon_{Ct}^{A}$ refer to growth rate in traditional TFP and TFP adjusted for scale economies, CU and mark-up respectively. Bias in TFP refers to the difference between growth rates in TFP and $-\varepsilon_{Ct}^{A}$.

The production process in the Indian paper industry also suggests certain technological improvements over time. Out of the three production technologies prevalent in the paper industry worldwide, viz., chemical, mechanical and thermo-mechanical, the thermo-mechanical method is found to be comparatively less-polluting, more productive and cost effective [World Bank 1992]. The share of the thermo-mechanical process in total output has recorded an increase over time in India. Based on the Food and Agricultural Association database [FAO], Pradhan and Barik (1999c) point out that highly polluting and less productive chemical-based production technology has declined from 92.4 per cent in 1976 to 78.7 per cent in 1992 in the Indian paper industry. Such a decline reflects technological improvements in the industry.

Table 8.2
Total Factor Productivity and Technological Progress Indices

Year	*TFP Index*	*TP Index*
1973-74	100.00	100.00
1974-75	95.11	88.93
1975-76	105.33	107.17
1976-77	105.15	112.64
1977-78	103.14	125.85
1978-79	101.66	125.52
1979-80	100.43	140.27
1980-81	100.15	144.26
1981-82	112.00	167.75
1982-83	89.37	149.66
1983-84	90.31	160.45
1984-85	93.28	192.82
1985-86	89.97	191.91
1986-87	91.20	202.94
1987-88	86.10	204.91
1988-89	87.21	220.71
1989-90	92.80	279.25
1990-91	94.54	308.95
1991-92	89.00	295.12
1992-93	83.09	279.05
1993-94	85.99	287.91
1994-95	86.67	339.81
1995-96	93.82	426.90
1996-97	88.01	427.48
1997-98	92.06	414.35

Improvement in TP could have come through the compliance to stricter environmental norms and openness that the industry has been subjected to. It may be recalled that various pollution regulation measures have been imposed over the years in the form of the Water Act (1974), Air Act (1981) and Environment Act (1986). These measures have required the industry to meet stricter emission norms. Empirical evidences in various countries have shown that environmental regulation is often associated with positive productivity growth [Pradhan and Barik 1999c; Wheeler *et al.* 1995; Hartman *et al.* 1997; Hettige *et al.* 1996]. Particularly, a positive relationship between scale and profitability (as competitiveness variables) and environment-improvement is shown in Hartman et al. (1997) and Hettige et al. (1996). Secondly, outward orientation or openness of an economy helps in the absorption of cleaner technology [Wheeler *et al.* 1995].

Structural Break in TP

Having established that TP in the paper industry is increasing, an attempt is made to examine the possibility of a structural break in its growth path. So TP in the industry was put to test for structural change over time by CUSUM-squared and sequential-Chow tests. The results of such an exercise, however, indicated no break in the growth rate. Thus, notwithstanding technological improvements in the industry over time, statistically significant change in the trend growth rate of TP did not come through in the wake of recent liberalisation measures.

The growth rate in TP index of the Indian paper industry, however, did not exhibit any structural break over the period of study. This could be because of a smooth change in the production process in the industry and gradual absorption of the shocks due to policy changes.

In this chapter we adjusted the traditional TFP index for non-fulfilment of constant returns to scale, full utilisation of capacity and marginal cost pricing. Based on the estimates of these characteristics, obtained earlier in Chapter 4, we adjusted the Solow residual. Such adjustment purged the effects of scale economies, capacity utilisation and mark-up from TFP. Thus the residual after the adjustment is ascribed to technological change and X-efficiency in the industry.

The findings of such an attempt showed substantial difference between the growth rate in TFP and technological progress. While traditional TFP exhibited a growth rate of -0.74 per cent per annum, a technological progress index constructed in a manner similar to TFP index showed an increase of 6.54 per cent per annum. No structural change in the TP index was found over the period, which showed that liberalisation during 1990s did not alter its long-term growth path.

The difference between negative TFP growth and positive TP growth could be ascribed to decline in the extent of scale economies and capacity utilisation in the industry. Moreover, increased use of cost effective and less-polluting technologies such as a thermo-mechanical process could have contributed to technological progress in the industry.

Notes

1. Such a relationship has been projected in the studies of Denny, Fuss and Waverman (1981), Morrison (1992) and Ohta (1974) in a full static equilibrium (FSE) framework.
2. In the case of imperfect competition, product market equilibrium is achieved when P_i is equal to marginal revenue product (MRP), i.e., marginal product multiplied by marginal revenue. Since in equilibrium MR = MC, $\frac{\partial f}{\partial X_i} = \frac{P_i}{\partial C/\partial Y}$ implies $\frac{\partial f}{\partial X_i} \cdot MC = P_i$, that is, $\frac{\partial f}{\partial X_i} \cdot MR = P_i$.

9

Summary and Conclusions

Obtaining a correct estimate of productivity and rate of change in it is quite important as it indicates the efficiency with which resources are utilised in an economy. In that sense productivity reflects the competitive strength of an industry and its general health.

TFP, which takes into account all the factors of production used in the production process, is a more comprehensive measure compared to partial productivity of inputs. It is given by the ratio of output to a weighted-combination of inputs. Under assumptions of constant returns to scale, full utilisation of capacity and presence of perfect competition it is equivalent, as pointed out by Solow, to technological change in an industry. However, in the case of violation of these assumptions TFP includes the effects of non-constant returns to scale, capacity utilisation and mark-up presenting in the process a biased measure of technological change.

The traditional TFP measure, often known as Solow residual, can be improved upon by incorporating appropriate adjustments in the method of estimation. Once we have estimates of scale economies, capacity utilisation and mark-up in the industry, the Solow residual can be modified to have these features of production structure. Consequently, the refined measure presents the effects of pure technological change on the productivity growth.

The present study undertakes an analysis of productivity performance of the Indian paper industry. The productive efficiency of the industry has not yet been scrutinised properly, even though it has undergone radical changes in policy environment after 1984-85. The controls on the industry during the decades of the sixties and seventies, which pervaded the spheres of production, distribution and pricing, were relaxed during the decades of the eighties and nineties. Due to these changes productivity performance of the industry is expected to record significant shifts, the nature and extent of which remain to be analysed as yet.

Studies in the area of productivity estimation mostly take the form of econometric estimation of a variable cost function. In this frame of analysis one could opt for either a partial static or partial dynamic equilibrium model. While a partial dynamic equilibrium model is sometimes employed to get the contribution of pure technological change in productivity, its formulation and estimation is besieged with problems, especially when the industry operates in a controlled policy regime. Therefore, many studies use a partial static equilibrium (PSE) framework while analysing productivity growth. In India, two studies have analysed the production structure following the above methodology. However, these studies have overlooked the aspects of possible imperfections in product market [Bharadwaj 1994] and capacity utilisation of capital input [Srivastava 1996]. Therefore, productivity estimation emanating from their analyses remained incomplete. The present study tried to include the features not considered by the methodology adopted by them.

In the present study we estimated the features of production structure in the Indian paper industry such as scale economies, economic capacity utilisation, mark-up over marginal cost and substitution elasticities. These characteristics were derived by using the parameters of a translog short-run variable cost function, in a PSE framework. The study covered the period 1973-74 to 1997-98 and used the data from the Annual Survey of Industries (ASI). In order to construct capital input, which has remained a debatable issue among empirical studies, we adopted the perpetual inventory method with the benchmark capital stock taken from Hashim and Dadi (1973). We allowed for four per cent depreciation so as to take care of wear and tear. Market rental of capital, which is not observed, was taken to be the sum of depreciation and long-term interest rates. As raw material was taken as one of the inputs in the study, we computed its price index by using structural coefficients given in the Input-Output Table, 1989. All the variables were deflated for price changes by relevant price indexes to the base 1981-82.

In order to derive production characteristics the study employed a cost function with four inputs, viz., capital, labour, energy and raw materials. Out of these, capital was taken to be a quasi-fixed factor, in the sense that it remained fixed in the short-run. The other inputs were considered to be variable in the sense that they could be adjusted to equilibrium levels within a single period. In order to obtain the parameters, we estimated a system of five equations, viz., variable cost, labour and energy shares, output share in a market equilibrium condition and inverse output demand. A non-linear maximum likelihood method was used to obtain the estimates.

To begin with, the underlying technology of the paper industry was evaluated through an econometric estimation of the translog variable cost function.

1. The estimated translog variable cost function was found to be well-behaved and had a good fit. It was observed to be increasing in output and variable input prices for all observations. While it could not fulfil the property that the estimated variable cost function should be decreasing in capital stock for 4 out of 25 observations, it was found to be convex in capital. In addition, concavity with respect to variable input prices was fulfilled at all observations. The R-squared between observed and predicted values of the cost and factor share equations had values of more than 0.90.
2. The rate of economic capacity utilisation in the Indian paper industry was observed to be less than unity as the average rate during 1973-98 was 75.45 per cent. Moreover, there was a general decline in the rate over time.
3. The industry was found to have exploited the benefits of scale economies during 1973-98. In the short-run degree of returns to scale varied between 1.87 in 1974-74 and 1.55 in 1981-82. On the other hand, long-run returns to scale varied between 1.55 in 1974-75 and 1.14 in 1995-96. The degree of long-run returns to scale showed

a decline over time.

4. The study estimated the mark-up over marginal cost in the industry to be 30.34 per cent. Thus pricing strategy in the industry has not followed the norms of perfect competition.
5. Analysis of the long-run APES between pairs of inputs indicated that all the variable inputs considered in the study, viz., labour, energy and material, were substitutes to one another.
6. Capital was found to be a complement to energy in the Indian paper industry. Keeping in view the fact that production process in the industry is energy intensive, *K-E* complementarity indicated difficulties in reducing the level of energy consumption through increased capital input. Moreover, an increase in price of energy is likely to retard the rate of investment in the industry. While a decrease in the price of energy would accelerate capital investment, it would be accompanied by additional energy demand.
7. The price elasticity of raw material was found to be more than unity in absolute terms for all the years. Such a result indicated that the industry would be sensitive to price changes in raw material.

In the process of estimating productivity growth, the study started with an estimation of TFP by the index number approach. The important findings of such an exercise are:

1. TFP in the Indian paper industry was found to have decreased from 100 in the year 1973-74 to 92.06 in 1997-98. Its trend growth turned out to be -0.74 per cent per annum, which is statistically significant at the 1 per cent level. The possibility of a structural break in the TFP series was not confirmed statistically.
2. An analysis of partial productivity of inputs exhibited improvements in labour productivity and a decrease in the case of others, viz., capital, energy and material. The improvement in labour productivity may be attributed to an increase in the capital-labour ratio.
3. Based on the estimates of a translog production function we decomposed the output growth into the contributions

of TFP and factor inputs. As a result, we found that TFP contributed negatively to output growth in the industry. While the combined contribution of inputs to output growth of the industry was found to be 101.15 per cent, TFP's share was -1.15 per cent. Among the individual inputs the raw material component contributed the maximum at 53.77 per cent while labour's share was the least at 5.45 per cent.

As the results of TFP estimation through the index number approach are considered unsatisfactory because of restrictive assumptions, we tried to purge the effects of scale economies, CU and mark-up from TFP growth. Such an exercise provided us with the contribution of pure technological progress to productivity growth.

Empirical estimation indicated a substantial difference between growth rates in TFP and technological progress (TP). While traditional TFP exhibited a growth rate of -0.74 per cent per annum, a TP index constructed in a manner similar to the TFP index showed an increase of 6.54 per cent per annum. In the process the present analysis could identify the bias in TFP growth, which was found to be -5.92 per cent. No structural change in the TP index was found over the period, which showed that liberalisation during the 1990s did not alter its long-term growth path.

The results of the study, however, need to be interpreted with caution because of the limitations associated with the database accessible to analysts. Some of the important limitations are the following:

The study covered a period of 25 years ranging 1973-74 to 1997-98 during which the quality of data used might have changed. Secondly, it was assumed that the inputs and output used in the production process did not undergo qualitative changes and maintained the same quality throughout. In fact, the proportion of output growth attributed to productivity could be affected by the qualitative improvements in inputs. Thirdly, infrastructural facilities such as highways and communication facilities play an important role in improving productivity. However, these intangible inputs are not included in the input bill of the industry. Fourthly, the ASI data, which are used in the study, suffer from non-reporting bias. Although it is a statutory requirement that all industrial units provide production operation data annually, many firms do not provide these on various grounds. Although non-reporting results in a simultaneous decline in the levels of output and inputs, it may affect productivity estimates to some extent. Notwithstanding the importance of the above limitations, it is pertinent to mention that most of these are concerned with the data source used by other studies using time series data.

Another major limitation of the study, which is equally relevant to others in the area, is its assumption of homogeneous capital input. By aggregating different components at historical prices, deflating these by a single index number and assuming all components to have a uniform rate of depreciation and longevity one may induce some amount of bias into the level of capital input. Moreover, the depreciation rate of 4 per cent per annum used by the present analysis is necessarily somewhat arbitrary, and based on value judgement that is unavoidable.

The deflator used for estimation of material input at constant prices also has certain limitations. The input-output table, which is used for the construction of the material input deflator is for both registered and unregistered sectors. As the I-O table is not available on the basis of such a differentiation, the study used it although the coverage of the paper industry taken for analysis is limited to the registered sector. Secondly, the limitation that structural change is not allowed when a single I-O table is used is applicable to the present study as well.

The output variable used in the study is at ex-factory prices, that is, exclusive of taxes. On the other hand, the WPI used as deflator of output is inclusive of taxes and subsidies. Thus, changes in tax rates may be influencing the rate of productivity growth. Moreover, the WPI data used as deflator may be suffering from non-reporting bias, apart from the error due to changes in weight when the base year is shifted.

Notwithstanding the above limitations, the study offers results which have important policy implications. Particularly, the contrast in growth rates of TFP and TP found in the case of the Indian paper industry helps identify the factors responsible for the observed decline in TFP. On the basis of the results of the present study the negative growth in TFP, in spite of technological progress, is due to a decline in scale economies and capacity utilisation. Thus policy measures to improve the productivity growth in the industry may have to arrest the current decline in degree of returns to scale and rate of capacity utilisation.

Bibliography

Ahluwalia, I. J., 1994, 'TFPG in Manufacturing Industry', *Economic and Political Weekly*, October 22, vol. 29, p.2836

Ahluwalia, I. J., 1991, *Productivity and Growth in Indian Manufacturing*, Oxford University Press, Delhi.

Ahluwalia, I. J., 1985, *Industrial Growth in India*, Oxford University Press, Delhi.

Ahuja, S. P., 1992, *Paper Industry in India*, Institute of Economic and Market Research, New Delhi.

Allen, R. G. D., 1938, *Mathematical Analysis for Economists*, Macmillan, London.

Applebaum, E., 1979a, 'On the Choice of Functional Forms', *International Economic Review*, vol. 20, no. 2, pp. 449-458.

Apte, P C, 1983, Substitution among Energy and Non-energy Inputs in Selected Indian Manufacturing Industries: An Econometric Analysis', *Indian Economic Journal*, 31, 2, Oct-Dec. 71-90.

Averech, H. and L. Johnson, 1962, 'Behaviour of the Firm under Regulatory Constraint', *American Economic Review*, vol. 52, no. 5, pp. 1052-69.

Balakrishnan, P. and K. Pushpangadan, 1998, 'What Do We Know about Productivity Growth in Indian Industry', *Economic and Political Weekly*, August 15, pp. 2241-6.

Banerjee, A., 1975, *Capital Intensity and Productivity in Indian Manufacturing*, Macmillan, Delhi.

Balakrishnan, P. and K. Pushpangadan, 1994, 'Total Factor Productivity Growth in Manufacturing Industry: A Fresh Look', *Economic and Political Weekly*, July 30, pp. 2028-35.

Barten, A. P., 1969, Maximum Likelihood Estimation of a Complete System of Demand Equations', *European Economic Review*, vol. 1, pp. 7-73.

Basant, R. and B. Fikkert, 1996, 'The Effects of R & D, Foreign Technology Purchase, and Domestic and International Spillovers on Productivity in Indian Firms, *The Review of Economics and Statistics*, vol. LXXVII, no. 2, May, pp. 187-99.

Bauer, P W, 1990, Recent Developments in the Econometric Estimation of Frontiers, *Journal of Econometrics*, vol. 46, pp. 39-56.

Berndt, E. R., 1991, *The Practice of Econometrics*, Addison-Wesley.

Berndt, E. R., 1976, 'Reconciling Alternative Estimates of the Elasticity of Substitution', *Review of Economics and Statistics*, vol. LVIII, no. 1, pp. 59-68.

Berndt, E. R. and L. R. Christensen (1974): 'Testing for Existence of a Consistent Aggregate Index of Labour Inputs', *American Economic Review*, Vol. LXIV, No.3.

Berndt, E. R, M. N. Darrough and W. E. Diewert, 1977, 'Flexible Functional Forms and Expenditure Distributions: An Application to Canadian Consumer Demand Functions', *International Economic Review*, vol. 18, no. 3, pp. 651-75.

Berndt, E. R. and B. C. Field (eds.), 1981, *Modeling and Measuring Natural Resource Substitution*, MIT Press, Cambridge.

Berndt, E. R. and M. A. Fuss, 1986, 'Productivity Measurement with Adjustments for Variations in Capacity Utilisation and other forms of Temporary Equilibrium', *Journal of Econometrics*, vol. 33, pp. 7-29.

Berndt E. R. and D. M. Hesse, 1986, 'Measuring and Assessing Capacity Utilisation in the Manufacturing Sector', *European Economic Review*, vol. 30, pp. 961-89.

Berndt, E. R. and M. S. Khaled, 1979, 'Parametric Productivity Measurement and Choice among Flexible Functional Forms', *Journal of Political Economy*, vol. 87, no. 6., pp. 1220-45.

Berndt, E. R. and C. J. Morrison, 1981, 'Capacity Utilization measures: Underlying Economic Theory and an Alternative Approach', *American Economic Review*, vol. 71, no. 2, pp. 48-52.

Berndt, E. R., C. J. Morrison and G. C. Watkins, 1979, Dynamic Models of Energy Demand: An Assessment and Comparison', in Berndt, E. R. and B. C. Field (eds.), 1981, *Modeling and Measuring Natural Resource Substitution*, MIT Press, Cambridge.

Berndt, E. R. and D. O. Wood, 1975, 'Technology, Prices, and Derived Demand for Energy', *The Review of Economics and Statistics*, vol. LVII, no.3, pp. 259-68.

Berndt, E. R. and D. O. Wood, 1979, 'Engineering and Economic Interpretations of Energy-Capital Complementarity', *American Economic Review*, vol. 69, June, pp. 342-54.

Berndt, E. R. and D. O. Wood, 1981, 'Engineering and Econometric Interpretations of Energy-Capital Complementarity: Reply and Further Results', *American Economic Review*, vol. 71, no. 5, pp. 1105-10.

Bharadwaj, R. N., 1994, *Some Economic Aspects of India's Iron and Steel Industry*, Ph. D. Thesis submitted to the University of Delhi.

Bhavani, D. A., 1991a, 'Factor Substitution and Factor Demand in Indian Modern Small Enterprises: A Case Study of Metal Products', *Artha Vijnana*, vol. 33, no. 1, pp. 41-55.

Bhavani, D. A., 1991b, 'Technical Efficiency in Indian Modern Small Scale Sector: An Application of frontier production', *Indian Economic Review*, vol. 26, no. 2, pp. 149-66.

Binswanger, H. P., 1974, 'The Measurement of Technological Change

Bias with Many Factors of Production', *American Economic Review*, vol. 64, no. 6, pp. 964-76.

Bischoff, C W and E C Kokkelenberg, 1987, Capacity utilisation and Depreciation-in-use, *Applied Economics*, vol. 19, pp. 995-1007.

Blades, D. W., 1991, 'Capital Measurement in OECD Countries: An Overview' in OECD (1991), *Technology and Productivity: The Challenge for Economic Policy*, Technology Programme, OECD, Paris.

Boskin, M. J. and L. J. Lau, 1990, *Post-war Economic Growth in the Group-of-Five Countries: A New Analysis*, Stanford University, Centre for Economic Policy Research, Technical Paper No. 217.

Brahmananda, P. R. (1982): *Productivity in the Indian Economy: Rising Inputs for Falling Outputs*, Himalaya Publishing House, Delhi.

Brahmananda, P. R. and V. R. Panchamukhi (eds.), *The Development Process of Indian Economy*, Himalaya Publishing House, Mumbai.

Brautigam R. R. and A F. Doughety, 1983, 'On the Estimation of Returns to Scale using Variable Cost Function', *Economics Letter*, vol. 11, pp. 25-31.

Brown, R. S. and L. R. Christensen, 1981, Estimating Elasticities of Substitution in a Model of Partial Static Equilibrium: An Application to U. S. Agriculture, in Berndt and Field (eds.), *Modeling and Measuring Natural Resource Substitution*, MIT Press.

Bruno, M., 1984, 'Raw Materials, Profits, and the Productivity Slowdown', *Quarterly Journal of Economics*, vol. XCIX, no. 1, pp. 1-29.

Burgess, D. F., 1975, 'Duality Theory and Pitfalls in Specification of Technology', *Journal of Econometrics*, vol. 33, pp. 105-21.

Cassels, J. H., 1937, 'Excess Capacity and Monopolistic Cornpetition', *Quarterly Journal of Economics*, vol. 51, pp. 426-43.

Caves, D. W. and L. R. Christensen, 1980, 'Global Properties of Flexible Functional Forms', *American Economic Review*, 70, 3, 422-432.

Caves D. W., L. R. Christensen and J. A. Swanson, 1981, 'Productivity Growth, Scale Economies and Capacity Utilisation in US Railroads, 1955-74', *American Economic Review*, vol. 71, no. 5, pp. 994-1002.

Chambers, R G, 1988, *Applied Production Analysis*, Cambridge University Press.

Chandhok, H. L., 1990, *India Data Base: The Economy*, Living Media Ltd., New Delhi.

Christensen, L. R. (1980), 'Discussion' on Diewert (1980), *American Economic Review*, vol. 70, no. 2, p. 279.

Christensen, L. R. and W. H. Greene (1976): 'Economies of Scale in U. S. Electric Power Generation', *Journal of Political Economy*, vol. 84, no. 1.

Christensen L. R., D. W. Jorgenson and L. J. Lau, 1971, 'Conjugate Duality and the Transcendental Logarithmic Production Function, *Econometrica*, vol. 39, no. 3, pp. 255-256.

Christensen L. R., D. W. Jorgenson and L. J. Lau, 1973, 'Transcendental Logarithmic Production Frontiers', *Review of Economics and Statistics*, vol. 55, no. 1, pp. 28-45.

Central Pollution Control Board (CPCB), 1991, *Comprehensive Industry Document for Large Pulp and Paper Industry*, New Delhi.

Copeland and Martin, 1938, 'The Correction of Wealth Income Estimates for Price Changes', in *Studies in Income and Wealth*, vol. 2, NBER, pp. 85-135.

CMIE (Centre for Monitoring of Indian Economy), 1999, *Industry: Market Size and Shares*, August.

Denny, M., 1974, 'The Relationship between Functional Forms for the Production System', *Canadian Journal of Economics*, vol. VII, no. 1, pp. 21-31.

Denison, 1964, 'The Unimportance of the Embodied Question', American Economic Review, vol. 54, no. 5, pp. 721-25.

Denny, M and M. Fuss, 1977, 'The Use of Approximation Analysis to Test for Separability and the Existence of Consistent Aggregates', *American Economic Review*, vol. 67, no. 3, pp. 404-18.

Denny, M., M. Fuss and L. Waverman, 1981, 'The Measurement and Interpretation of Total Factor Productivity, in Regulated Industries, with an application to Canadian Telecommunications', in T. G. Cowing and R. E. Stevenson (eds.), *Productivity Measurement in Regulated Industries*, Academic Press, New York.

Diewert, W. E., 1971, 'An Application of Shephard Duality Theorem: A Generalized Leontief Production Function', *Journal of Political Economy*, vol. 79, pp. 481-507.

Diewert, W. E., 1973, 'Functional Forms for Profit and Transformation Functions, Journal of Economic Theory, vol. 6, no. 3, pp. 284-316.

Diewert, W. E., 1976, 'Exact and Superlative Index Numbers', *Journal of Econometrics*, vol. 4, pp. 115-45.

Diewert, W. E., 1980, 'Capital and the Theory of Productivity Measurement', *American Economic Review*, vol. 70, no. 2, pp. 260-7.

Diewert, W. E. and T. J. Wales, 1987, 'Flexible Functional Forms and Global Curvature Conditions', *Econometrica*, 55, 1, pp. 43-68.

Dholakia, B. H. and R. H. Dholakia, 1994, 'Total Factor Productivity Growth in Indian Manufacturing', *Economic and Political Weekly*, December 31, pp. 3342-4.

Dogramaci A. and R. Fare (eds.), 1988, *Applications of Modern Production Theory: Efficiency and Productivity*, Kluwer Academic Publishers.

Epstein, L. and M. Denny, 1980, 'Endogenous Capital Utilisation in a Short-Run production Model', *Journal of Econometrics*, vol. 12, pp. 189-207.

Felipe, J. (1997): *Total Factor Productivity Growth in East Asia: A Critical Survey*, EDRC Report Series No. 65, Asian Development Bank, Economics and Development Resource Centre.

Field, B. C. and E. R. Berndt, 1981, 'An Introductory Review of Research on the Economics of Natural Resource Substitution, in Berndt and Field (eds.), *Modelling and Measuring Natural Resource Substitution*, MIT Press, Cambridge.

Fisher, I., 1927, *The Making of Index Numbers*, Houghton-Mifflin, Boston.

Food and Agricultural Association (FAO), *Pulp and Paper Capacities* (various issues), Geneva.

Forsund, F., K. Lovell and P. Schmidt, 1980, 'A Survey of Frontier Production Function and their Relationship to Efficiency Measurement', *Journal of Econometrics*, vol. 13, May, pp. 5-25.

Friedlander, A. and R. Spady, 1981, *Freight Transport Regulation: Equity, Efficiency and Competition in the rail and Trucking Industries*, MIT Press, Cambrdge.

Fuss, M. and d. McFadden (eds.), 1978, *Production Economics: A Dual Approach to Theory and Applications*, vol. 1, North-Holland.

Gangopadhyay, S. and N. Wadhwa, 1998, 'Economic Reforms and Labour', *Economic and Political Weekly*, May 30.

Goldar, B. N., 2000, *Productivity Growth in Indian Manufacturing in the 1980s and 1990s*, Institute of Economic Growth, Delhi.

Goldar, B. N., 1986, *Productivity Growth in Indian Industry*, Allied Publishers, New Delhi.

Goldar, B. N., 1985, 'Unit Size and Economic Efficiency in Small Scale Soap Industry', *Arthavijnana*, vol. 27, no. 1, pp. 21-40.

Goldar, B N, 1992, Productivity and Factor Use Efficiency in Indian Industry, in A. Ghosh et al. (eds.), *Indian Industrialization, Structure and Policy Issues,* Oxford University Press, Delhi.

Goldar, B. N. and V S Renganathan, 1991, 'Capacity Utilisation in Indian industries', *Indian Economic Journal*, 39, 2, pp. 65-78.

Good, D. H., M. I. Nadiri and R. C. Sickles (1997), 'Index Number and Factor Demand Approaches to the Estimation of Productivity', in Pesaran, M. H. and P. Schmidt (eds.), *Handbook of Applied Econometrics*, vol. II, North-Holland.

Government of India, 1999, *Guide to Official Statistics*, CSO, Department of Statistics, Government of India, New Delhi.

Government of India, 1997, *Annual Report 1996-97*, Ministry of Environment and Forest, New Delhi.

Government of India, 1995, *A Technical Note to the Eighth Plan of India (1992-97)*, Planning Commission, New Delhi.

Government of India (a), *Annual Survey of Industries: Summary Results for Factory Sector* (various issues), Central Statistical Organisation, Ministry of Planning, New Delhi.

Government of India (b), *Index Numbers of Wholesale Prices* (various issues), Ministry of Industry, New Delhi.

Government of India (c), *Economic Survey* (various issues), Ministry of Finance, Economic Division, New Delhi

Government of India (d), Input- Output Table (various issues), Ministry of Planning, New Delhi.

Greene, W. H., 1997, 'Frontier Production Functions', in Pesaran, M. H. and P. Schmidt (eds.), *Handbook of Applied Econometrics*, vol. II, North-Holland

Greene, W. H., 1990, *Econometric Analysis*, Macmillan, New York.

Griffin, J. M., 1981, 'The Energy-Capital Complementarity Controversy: A progress report on Reconciliation Attempts', in Berndt and Field (eds.), *Modelling and Measuring Natural Resource Substitution*, MIT Press, Cambridge.

Griffin J. M. and P. R. Gregory, 1976, 'An Inter-country Translog Model of Energy Substitution Responses', *American Economic Review*, vol. 66, December, pp. 845-57.

Griliches, Z., 1996, 'The Discovery of the Residual: A Historical Note', *Journal of Economic Literature*, vol. XXXIV, 1324-1330.

Griliches, Z. and V. Ringstad, 1971, *Economies of scale and the Form of Production Function*, North-Holland.

Gujarati, D. N., 1988, *Basic Econometrics*, Mc Graw Hill.

Hall, R. E., 1968, 'Technical Change and Capital from the Point of View of the Dual', *Review of Economics Studies*, vol. 35, pp. 34-46.

Hall, R. E., 1988, 'The Relation between Price and marginal Cost in U. S. Industry', *Journal of Political Economy*, vol. 96, no. 5, pp. 921-47.

Hall, R. E., 1990, Invariance Properties of Solow's Productivity Residual', in Diamond, P. (ed.), *Growth/Productivity/ Unemployment*, The MIT Press.

Hall, R. E. and D. W. Jorgenson, 1967, 'Tax Policy and Investment Behaviour', *American Economic Review*, vol. 57, no. 3, pp. 391-414.

Hamermesh, D S and G A Pfann, 1996, 'Adjustment Costs in Factor Demand', *Journal of Economic Literature*, XXXIV, 3, 1264-1292.

Hartman, R. S., M. Huq and D. Wheeler, 1997, *Why Paper Mills Clean Up: Determination of Pollution Abatement in Four Asian Countries*, Policy Research Working Paper 1710, The World Bank, Policy Research Department.

Hashim, S. R. and M. M. Dadi, 1973, *Capital-Output Relations in Indian Manufacturing*, M. S. University, Baroda.

Hazilla, M. and R. J. Kopp, 1986, Testing For Separable Functional Structure using Temporal equilibrium Models, *Journal of Econometrics*, vol. 33, pp. 119-141.

Hercowitz, Z., 1998, 'The Embodiment Hypothesis: A Review Essay', *Journal of Monetary Economics*, vol. 41, no. 1, pp. 217-224.

Hettige, H., M. Huq, S. Pargal, and D. Wheeler, 1996, 'Determinants of Pollution Abatement in Developing Countries: Evidence from South and Southeast Asia', *World Development*, vol. 24, no. 12.

Hotelling, H., 1932, 'Edgeworth's Taxation Paradox and the Nature of Demand and Supply Function', *Political Economy*, vol. 40, pp. 577-616.

Hulten, C. R, 1992, 'Growth Accounting when Technical Change is Embodied in Capital', *American Economic Review*, vol. 82, pp. 964-80.

Hulten, C. R. and S. Srinivasan, 1999, 'Indian Manufacturing Industry: Elephant or Tiger?', *NBER Working Paper* 7441, NBER.

Jha R, M N Murty and B S Sahni, 1992, Technical efficiency in the Public Sector: An Analysis of the State Electricity Boards in India, *Indian Economic Review*, 385-395.

Jha, R., M. N. Murty and S. Paul, 1991, 'Technological Change, Factor Substitution and Economies of Scale in Selected Manufacturing Industries in India', *Journal of Quantitative Economics*, Vol.7.

Jha, R., M. N. Murty, S. Paul and B. B. Rao, 1993, An Analysis of Technological change, Factor Sustitution and Economies of Scale in Manufacturing Industries in India, *Applied Econometrics*, 25, 1337-1343.

Jorgenson, D. W., 1966, 'The Embodiment Hypothesis', *Journal of Political Economy*, vol. 74, no. 1, pp. 1-17.

Jorgenson, D. W., 1986, 'Econometric Methods for Modelling Producer Behaviour', in Griliches and Intriligator (eds.), *Handbook of Econometrics*, vol. III, North-Holland.

Jorgenson, D. W., 1990, 'Productivity and Economic Growth', in Berndt and Triplett (eds.), *Fifty Years of Economic Measurement*, National Bureau of Economic Research (NBER), New York.

Jorgenson, D. W., F. M. Gollop and B. Fraumeni, 1987, *Productivity and U. S. Economic Growth*, North-Holland, Amsterdam.

Jorgenson D. W. and Z. Griliches, 1967, 'The Explanation of Productivity Change, *Review of Economic Studies*, vol. 34, pp. 249-283.

Judge, et al. 1988, *Introduction to Theory and Practice of Econometrics*, Wiley, Second Edition.

Kang, H. and G. M. Brown, 1981, 'Partial and Full Elasticities of Substitution and the Energy-Capital Complementarity Controversy', in Berndt and Field (eds.), *Modeling and Measuring Natural Resource Substitution*, MIT Press.

Kendrick, J. W., 1961, *Productivity Trends in the United States*, National Bureau of Economic Research (NBER), Princeton Press, Princeton.

Kennedy, C and A P Thirlwal, 1972, 'Surveys in Applied Economics: Technical Progress', *The Economic Journal*, March, pp. 11-72

Kim, M. and A. Sachis, 1986, 'The Structure of Production, Technological Change and Productivity in a Port', *Journal of Industrial Economics*, vol. XXXV, no. 2, pp. 209-23.

Klein, L. R., 1960, Some Theoretical Issues in the Measurement of Capacity, *Econometrica*, vol. 28, pp. 272-86.

Krishna, K. L., 1987, 'Industrial Growth and Productivity in India', in Brahmananda, P. R. and V. R. Panchamukhi (eds.), *The Development Process of Indian Economy*, Himalaya Publishing House, Mumbai.

Krugman, P., 1994, 'The Myth of Asia's Miracle', *Foreign Affairs*, November/December.

Kulatilaka, N., 1987, 'The Specification of Partial Static Equilibrium Models', *Review of Economics and Statistics*, vol. LXIX, no. 2, pp. 327-35.

Kulatilaka, N., 1985, 'Tests on Validity of Static Equilibrium Models', *Journal of Econometrics*, vol. 28, pp. 253-68.

Lau, L. J., 1976, 'A Characterization of the Normalized Restricted Profit Function', *Journal of Economic Theory*, vol. 12, pp. 131-163.

Lau, L. J., 1978, 'Applications Profit Functions', in Fuss and McFadden (eds.), *Production Economics: A Dual Approach to Theory and Applications*, vol. 1, North-Holland.

Lau, L. J., 1986, 'Functional Forms in Econometric Modelling',

Handbook of Econometrics, vol. 3, North-Holland.

Lau L. J. and P. A. Yotopoulos, 1971, 'A Test of Relative Efficiency and Application to Indian Agriculture', *American Economic Review*, pp. 94-108.

Majumdar, S. K., 1996, 'Fall and Rise of Productivity in Indian Industry', *Economic and Political Weekly*, November 30.

McIntosh, J, 1982, 'Dynamic Interrelated Factor Demand Systems: the United Kingdom 1950-78', *Economic Journal*, Supplement on Conference Papers, vol. 93, pp. 79-85.

Mitra, A., A. Varoudakis and M. A. Veganzones, 1998, State Infrastructure and Productive Performance in Indian Manufacturing, Technical Paper No. 139, OECD Development Centre.

Mitra, 1999, 'Total Factor Productivity Growth and Technical Efficiency in Indian Industries', *Economic and Political Weekly*, July 31, 1999, pp. M98-M105.

Morrison, C. J., 1986, 'Productivity Measurement with Non-Static Expectations and Varying Capacity Utilization: An Integrated Approach', Journal of Econometrics, 33, 51-74.

Morrison, C. J., 1988a, 'Quasi-Fixed Inputs in U. S. and Japanese Manufacturing: A Generalized Leontief Restricted Cost Function Approach', *Review of Economics and Statistics*, vol. LXX, no. 2, pp. 275-87.

Morrison, C. J., 1988b, 'Subequilibrium in the North American Steel Industries: A Study of Short-run Biases from Regulation and Utilization Fluctuation, *Economic Journal*, June, pp. 390-411.

Morrison, C. J., 1988c, 'Capacity Utilization and Productivity Measurement: An Application to the U. S. Automobile Industry', in Dogramaci and Fare (eds.), *Applications of Modern Production Theory: Efficiency and Productivity*, Kluwer Academic Publishers.

Morrison, C. J., 1992, 'Unravelling the Productivity Growth Slowdown in the United States, Canada and Japan: The Effects of Subequilibrium, Scale Economies and Markups', *The Review of Economics and Statistics*, vol. LXXIV, No. 3.

Morrison C J and E R Berndt, 1981, Short-run Labour productivity in a Dynamic Model, *Journal of Econometrics*, vol. 16, pp. 339-365.

Nadiri, M. I., 1982, 'Producers Theory', in Arrow, K. J. and M. D. Intriligator (eds.), *Handbook of Mathematical Economics*, vol. II, North-Holland.

Nadiri, M. I. and S. Kim, 1996, *Production Structure and Productivity Growth: A Comparison of U. S., Japanese and Korean Manufacturing Sectors*, National Bureau of Economic Research (NBER) Working Paper 5506, National Bureau of Economic Research.

Nadiri, M. I. And B. Nandi, 1999, 'Technical Change, Mark-up, Divesture and Productivity Growth in the U. S. Telecommunication Industry', *Review of Economics and Statistics*, vol. 81, no. 3, pp. 488-98.

Nagaraj, R, 1999, 'How Good are India's Industrial Statistics', *Economic and Political Weekly*, February 6, pp. 350-5.

Nelson, R. A., 1989, 'On the Measurement of Capacity Utilisation, The Journal of Industrial Economics, vol. XXXVII, no. 3, pp.273-86.

Nemoto, J., Y. Nakanishi and S. Madano, 1993, Scale Economies and Over-Capitalization in Japanese Electric Utilities, International Economic Review, vol. 34, no. 2, pp. 431-40.

OECD, 1991, *Technology and Productivity: The Challenge for Economic Policy*, Technology Programme, OECD, Paris.

Ohta, M., 1974, 'A Note on the Duality between Production and Cost Functions: Rate of Returns to Scale and Rate of Technical Progress, *Economic Studies Quarterly*, vol. 25, pp. 63-65.

Panda, H., 1998, *An Economic Analysis of the Road Transport Vehicle Industry in India*, Ph. D. Thesis submitted to the University of Delhi.

Park, S. R. and J. K. Kwon, 1995, 'Rapid Economic Growth with Increasing Returns to Scale Little or No Productivity growth', *Review of Economics and Statistics*, Vol. LXXVII.

Paul, S., 1974, Growth and Utilisation in Industrial Capacity, *Economic and Political Weekly*, vol. IX, no. 49, Dec. 7, 2025-2032.

Pesaran, M. H. and P. Schmidt (1997), *Handbook of Applied Econometrics*, vol. II, North-Holland.

Pindyck, R. S. and J. J. Rotemberg, 1983, 'Dynamic Factor Demands and the Effects of Energy Price Shocks', *American Economic Review*, vol. 73, no. 5, pp. 1066-79.

Poirier, D., 1974, *The Econometrics of Structural Change*, North-Holland, Amsterdam.

Pradhan, B. K. and M. R. Saluja, 1998, 'Industrial Statistics in India: Sources, Limitations and Data Gaps', *Economic and Political Weekly*, 33, 21, May 23.

Pradhan, G. and K. Barik, 1998, 'Fluctuating Total Factor Productivity in India: Evidence from Selected Polluting Industries', *Economic and Political Weekly*, February 28.

Pradhan, G. and K. Barik, 1999a, "Sustainability of Output Growth in Indian Manufacturing: A Decomposition Analysis of Selected Industries', paper presented at presented at 35th Annual Conference of the Indian Econometric Society at Rajasthan University, Jaipur, March 11-13, 1999, and at the 1999 Meeting of the Australasian Econometric Society, University of Technology, Sydney, July 7-9, 1999.

Pradhan, G. and K. Barik, 1999b, 'Total Factor Productivity Growth in Developing Economies: A Study of Selected Industries in India ', *Economic and Political Weekly*, July 31, 1999, pp. M92-M97.

Pradhan, G. and K. Barik, 1999c, 'Environment-Friendly Behaviour and Competitiveness: A Study of Pulp and Paper Industry of India', *Environmental and Resource Economics*, vol. 14, no. 4, pp. 481-501.

Prucha, I R and M I Nadiri, 1996, Endogenous Capital Utilisation and Productivity Measurement in Dynamic Factor Demand Models: Theory and Application to the US Electrical Machinery Industry, *Journal of Econometrics*, vol. 71, pp. 343-379.

Ramaswamy, K. V., R. R. Vaidya, R. J. Bennis and J. G. M. Hoogeveen, 1996, 'Input Substitution in the Indian Paper Industry: a Variable Cost Function Approach', *CREED Working Paper No. 7*, International Institute of Environment and Development (ILED).

Rao, J. M., 1996, 'Manufacturing Productivity Growth: Method and Measurement', *Economic and Political Weekly*, November 2, pp. 2927-36.

Reserve bank of India (RBI) (a), *Report on Currency and Finance, vol. I*, (various issues), Mumbai.

Reserve bank of India (RBI), 1988, *Report on Currency and Finance, vol. I*, Mumbai.

Samuelson, P. A., 1953, 'Prices of Factors and Goods in General Equilibrium', *Review of Economic Studies*, vol. 21, no. 1, pp. 1-20.

Sargan, J. D., 1971, 'Production Functions', in Layard et al., *Qualified Manpower and Economic Performance*, Penguin Press, London.

Sato, R and R. Ramachandran, 1980, 'Measuring the Impact of Technical Progress on the Demand for Intermediate Goods: A Survey', *Journal of Economic Literature*, vol. XVIII, pp. 1003-1024.

Schankerman, M. and M. I. Nadiri, 1986, 'A Test of Static Equilibrium Models and Rates of Returns to Quasi-Fixed factors, with an Application to the Bell System', *Journal of Econometrics*, vol. 33, pp. 97-118.

Shephard, R. W., 1953, *Cost and Production Functions*, Princeton University Press, Princeton.

Solow, R. M., 1957, 'Technical Change and the Aggregate production Function', *Review of Economics and Statistics*, vol. 39, no. 3, pp. 312-20.

Srivastava, V., 1996, *Liberalization, Productivity and Competition: A Panel Study of Indian Manufacturing*, Oxford University Press, Delhi.

Srivastava, V., 2000, *Impact of Economic Reforms on Industrial Productivity, Efficiency and Competitiveness: A Panel Study of Indian Companies*, National Council of Applied Economic Research, New Delhi.

Stevenson, R., 1980, 'Measuring Technological Bias', *The American Economic Review*, March, vol. 70, no. 1, pp. 162-173.

Stigler, G. J., 1947, *Trends in Output and Employment*, National Bureau of Economic Research (NBER).

Subbarao, K. G. K., 1999, *Some Areas of Data – Perspectives on Interpretations*, paper presented at the 35th Annual Conference of the Indian Econometric Society, March 11-13, University of Rajasthan, Jaipur.

Tinbergen, J., 1942, 'Zur Theorie der Langfristigen Wirtschaftsentwicklung', *Weltwirtshaftliches Archiv*, vol. 55, no. 1, pp. 511-49.

Trivedi, P., A. Prakash and D. Sinate, 2000, *Productivity in Major Manufacturing Industries in India: 1973-74 to 1997-98*, DRG Study, Reserve Bank of India, Mumbai.

Uzawa, H., 1962, 'Production Functions with Constant Elasticity of Substitution', *Review of Economic Studies*, vol. 29, pp. 291-99.

Wales, T. J., 1977, 'On the Flexibility of Flexible functional forms: An Empirical Approach', *Journal of Econometrics*, vol. 5, pp. 183-93.

Wheeler, D., M. Huq and P. Martin, 1995, *Process Change, Economic Policy and Industrial Pollution*, Mimeo, The World Bank.

White, K. J., 1990, *SHAZAM: User's Reference Manual*, Version 6.2, Ronalds Printing, Canada.

Williams, M. and P. S. Laumas, 1984, 'The Relation between Energy and Non-energy inputs in India's Manufacturing', *Journal of Industrial Economics*, vol. 30, no. 2, pp. 113-22.

World Bank, 1992, *World Development Report*, Oxford University Press.

Index